MW01701501

30 INTERNATIONAL DESIGNERS INTERPRET THE BICYCLE AND OUR PUBLIC WORLD

PUBLIC WORKS

"THE FREEDOM TO MAKE AND REMAKE OUR CITIES AND OURSELVES IS, I WANT TO ARGUE, ONE OF THE MOST PRECIOUS YET MOST NEGLECTED OF OUR HUMAN RIGHTS."
– DAVID HARVEY

This publication accompanies the launch of PUBLIC WORKS, a design project inaugurated by a traveling poster exhibition in October 2012 in San Francisco and New York. We recruited over 25 world-renowned designers and illustrators to design posters around the concept of "public." All of the posters are represented in this publication.

The impetus for PUBLIC WORKS is to bring greater attention to the critical issues of public space, access, and livability of our cities. In recent decades, our cities have been evolving from manufacturing and industrial centers into cultural hubs. The 20th Century movement that encouraged people to leave cities for the suburbs has now been reversed. For the first time in our history the majority of the world's population lives in cities, and this trend appears irreversible. The influx of intellectual capital and diversity can be seen in cities across the United States.

People choose cities for what they offer: connections with people, ideas, stimulation, opportunity, creativity, and diversity. Our public spaces should facilitate these connections, not stifle them. The stakes are high—will we live in cities that welcome and excite us, places that we take pride in, or will we accept the problems that we've become accustomed to? Our ability to manage this development will be one of the ways our civilization is judged.

We believe that more of our urban streets and sidewalks should be reclaimed for walking and bicycling, and that our public spaces should be developed for better human interaction and conversation. We'd like to see intimate connections between residences and shops, parks, cafes, libraries, and friendly streets safe enough for kids and older folks to get around on foot or on a bicycle. The quality and usage of our public spaces is the measure of the success of our democracy. They are the only places where all members of society can congregate—regardless of economic or social status. It is in our public spaces that we are exposed to our pluralistic society on equal footing. It's where we become us.

Positive change with respect to the value of public space has been building momentum around the world over the last few decades. The "Livable Cities" movement began in Europe, but many cities in the US have been following suit. We have dramatic, high profile examples in the US ranging from The High Line in New York to Millennium Park in Chicago to San Francisco's Embarcadero. Everyday examples are occurring in many cities. Bike share programs that are common in Europe have been introduced in Washington DC and elsewhere.

An increasing number of bike lanes can been found in almost all cities across the US, with New York becoming an international exemplar. Cities as diverse as Minneapolis and Portland are vying for "most bikable city" honors in the US. Even car-centric modern cities like Los Angeles are implementing numerous alternative transportation solutions. The 21st Century will hopefully become the century known for enlightened urban development of our modern world.

Many of the key issues for our cities and our public world are often overlooked, taken for granted, and even contested. Design can help make these issues more visual, obvious, and understandable. Posters have a longstanding tradition of focusing attention on important issues in the public arena, often displayed in store windows, pedestrian walkways, subway walls, and bus shelters. These posters should help to do the same, from angles as varied and diverse as the designers themselves.

We thank the designers for their inspirational
and unique Public Works.

Rob Forbes
Founder of PUBLIC and
Design Within Reach

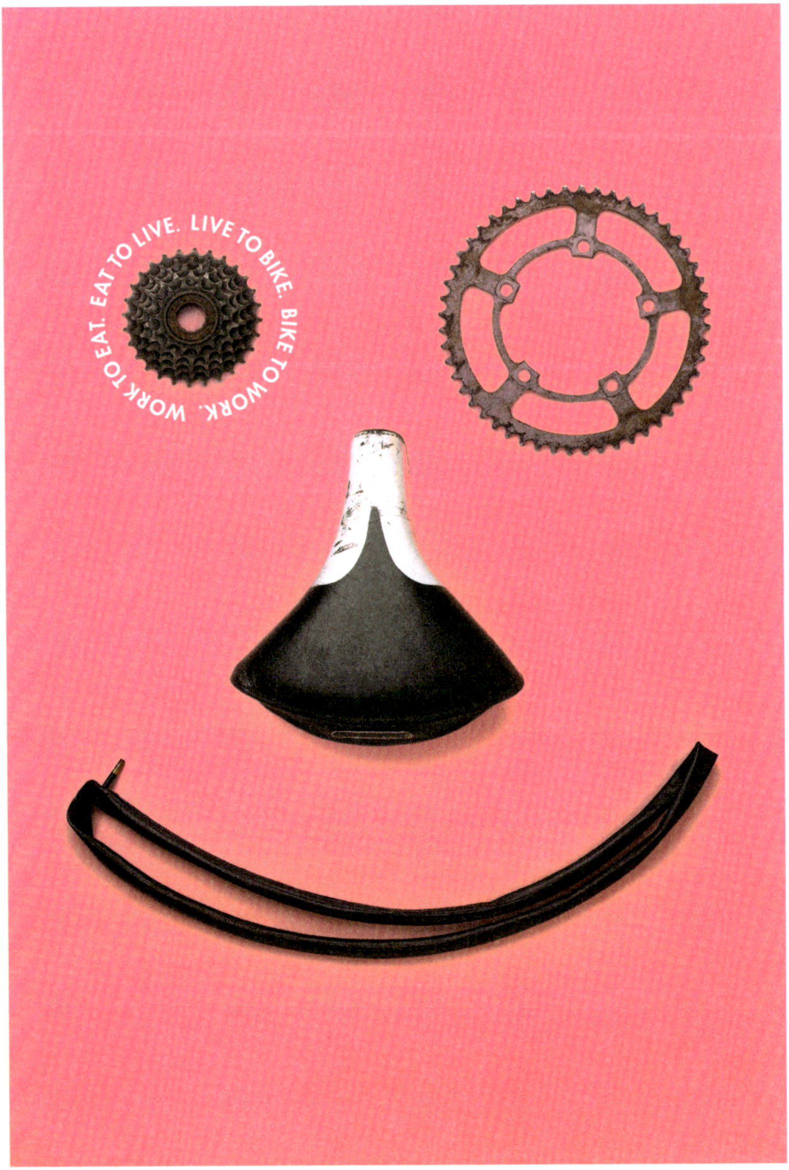

DANA ARNETT

I relax by taking my bicycle
apart and putting it back together again.
Michelle Pfeiffer

PUBLIC WORKS

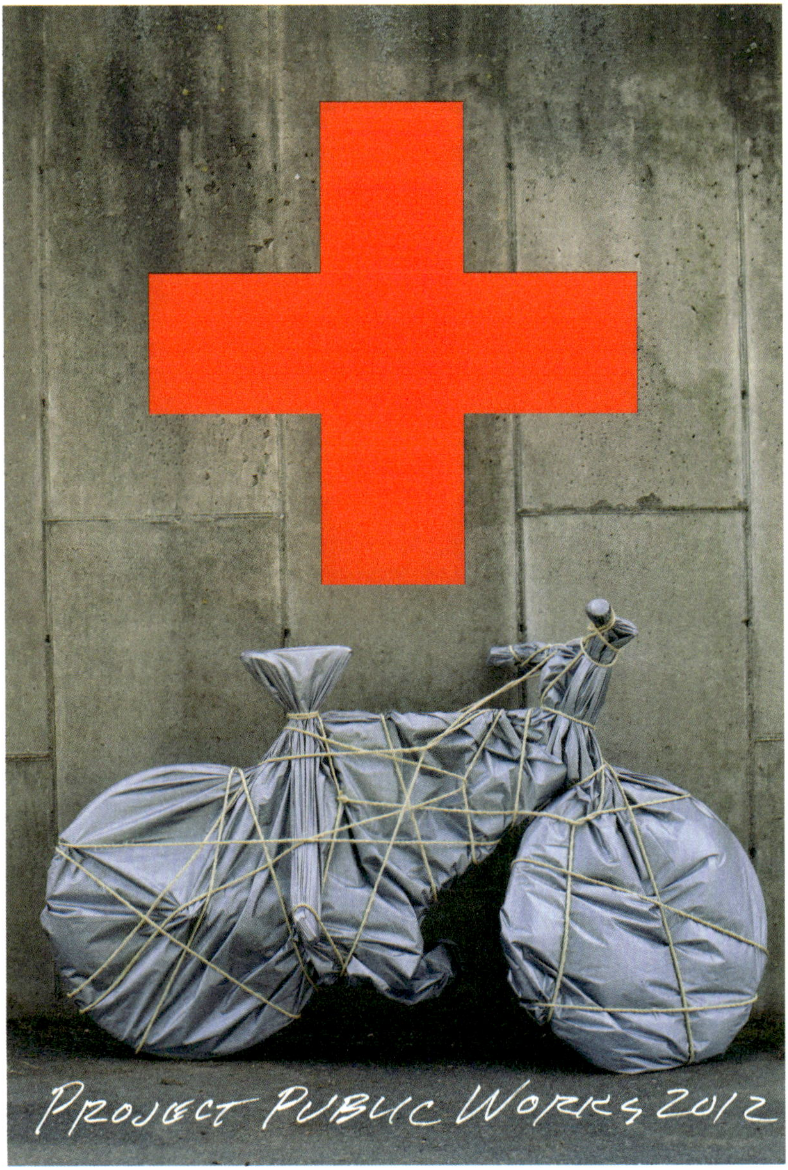

JOHN BIELENBERG

Forget the damned motor car
and build the cities for lovers and friends.
Lewis Mumford

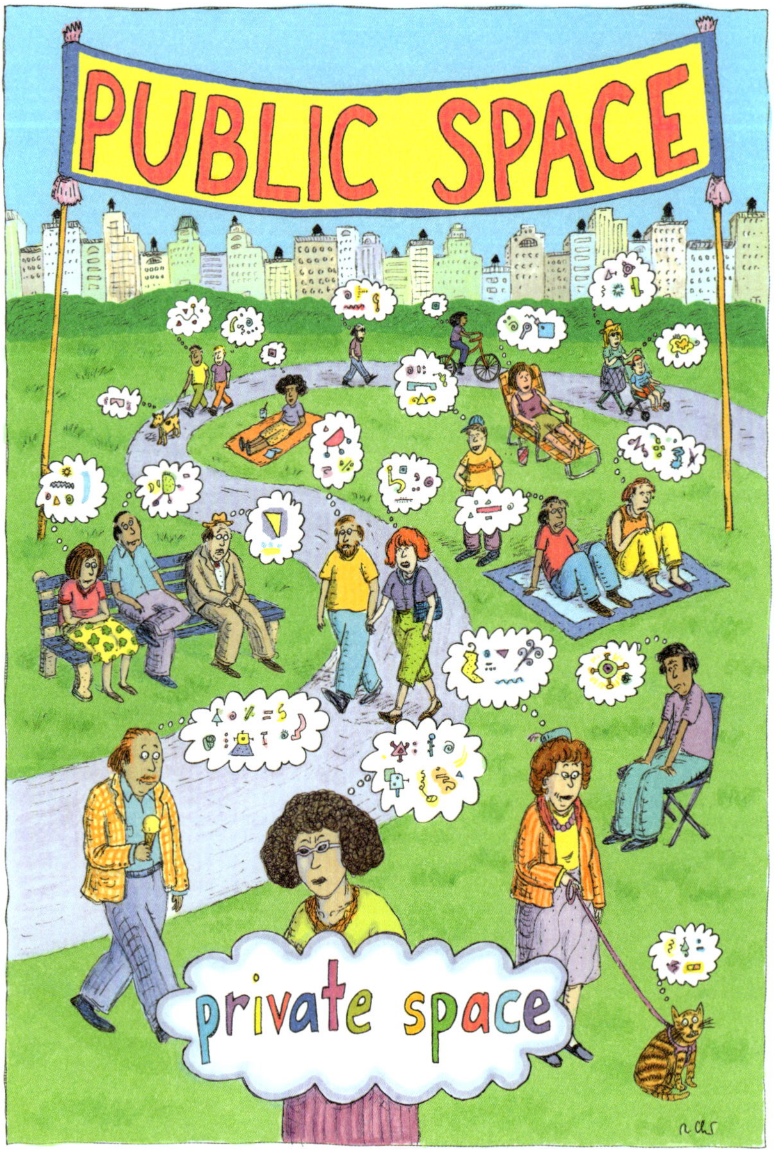

ROZ CHAST

The ballet of the good city sidewalk never
repeats itself from place to place, and in any one place
is always replete with new improvisations.

Jane Jacobs

PUBLIC WORKS

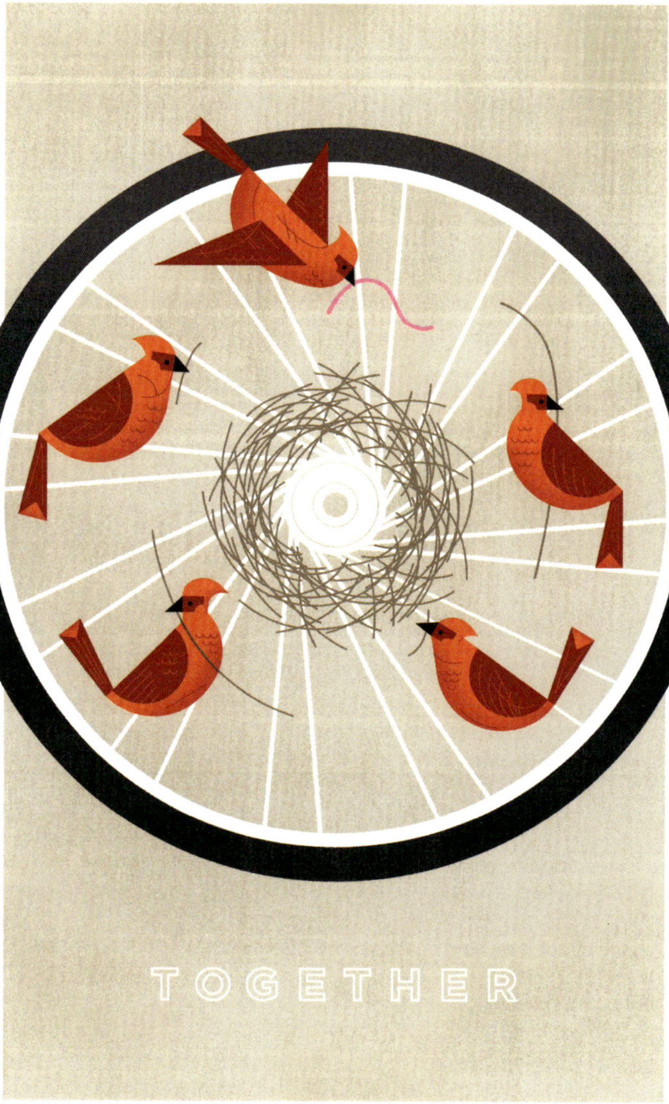

FRANK CHIMERO

The bicycle, the bicycle surely,
should always be the vehicle of novelists and poets.

Christopher Morley

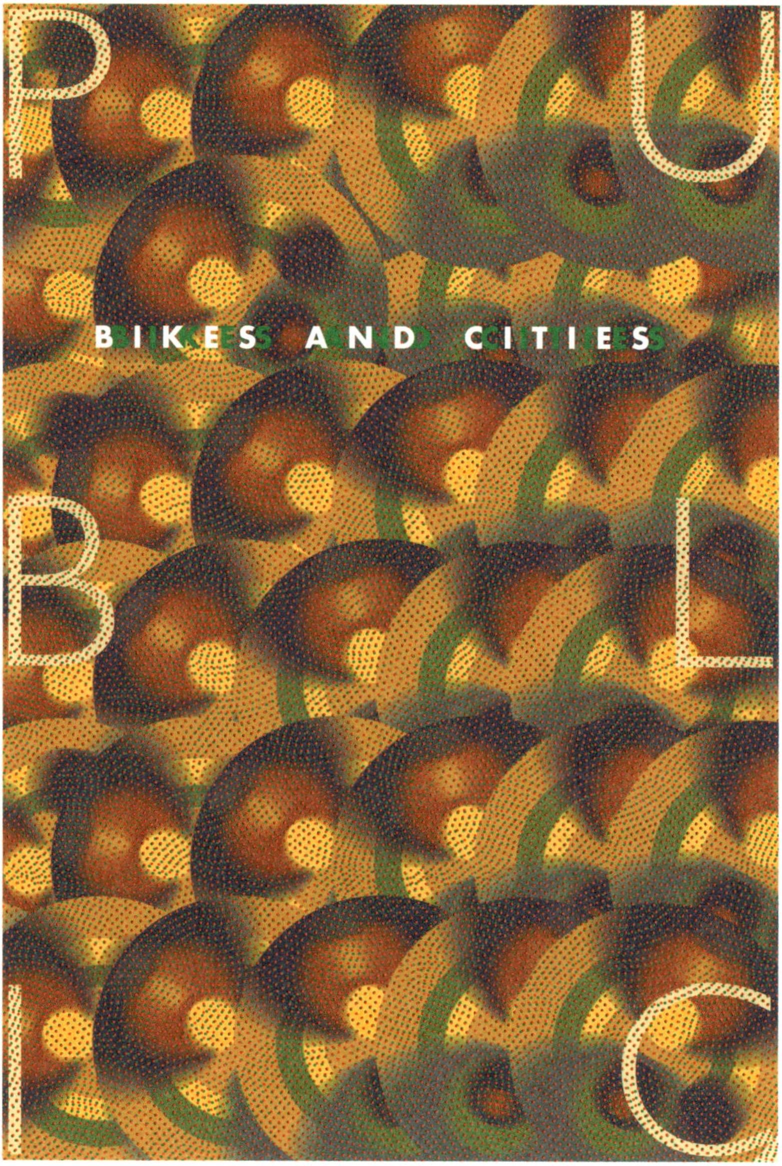

MILTON GLASER

The chief function of the city
is to convert power into form, energy into culture,
dead matter into the living symbols
of art, biological reproduction into social creativity.
Lewis Mumford

PUBLIC WORKS

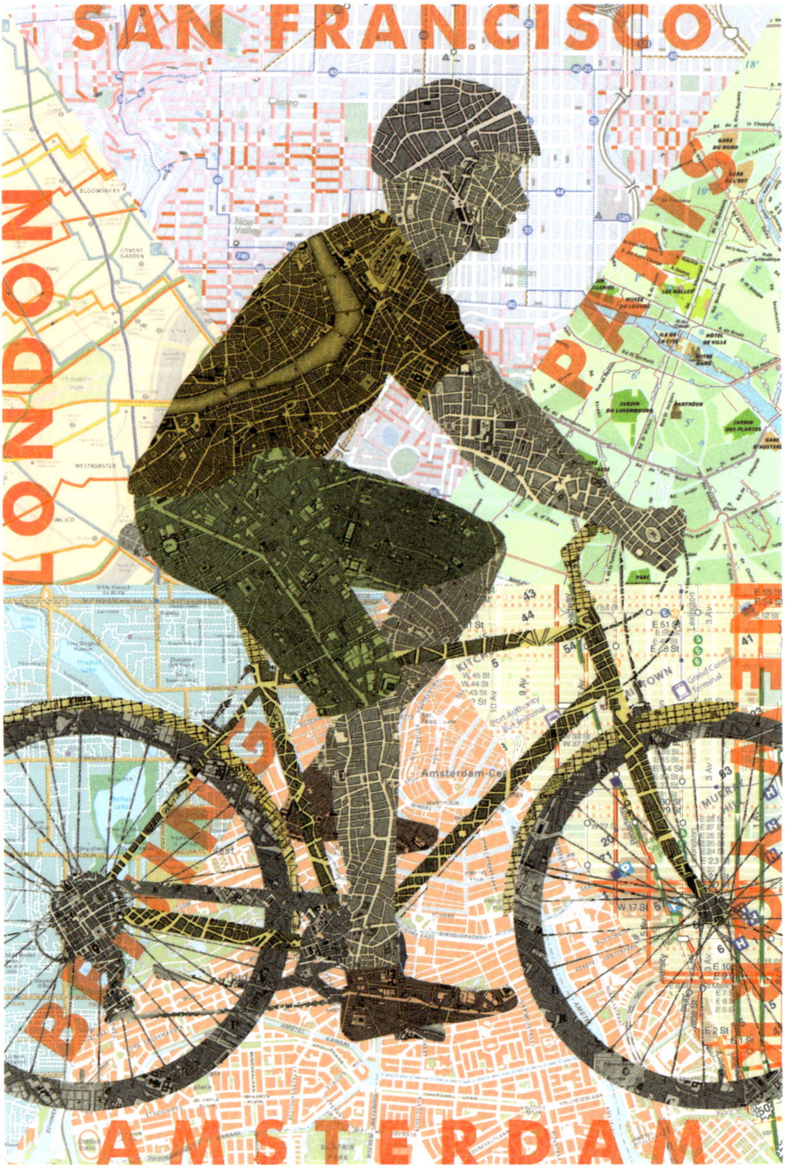

KIT HINRICHS

A good city can be defined
as one where we want to be out in Public space.
Jan Gehl

PUBLIC WORKS

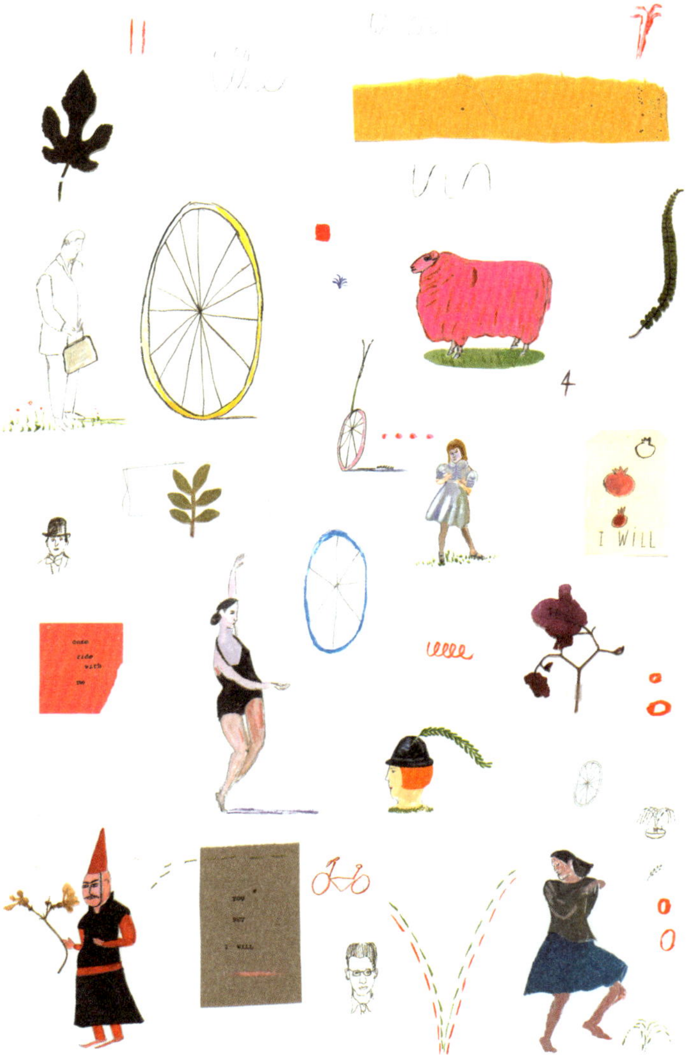

MAIRA KALMAN

The bicycle has done more for the
emancipation of women than anything else in the world.

Susan B. Anthony

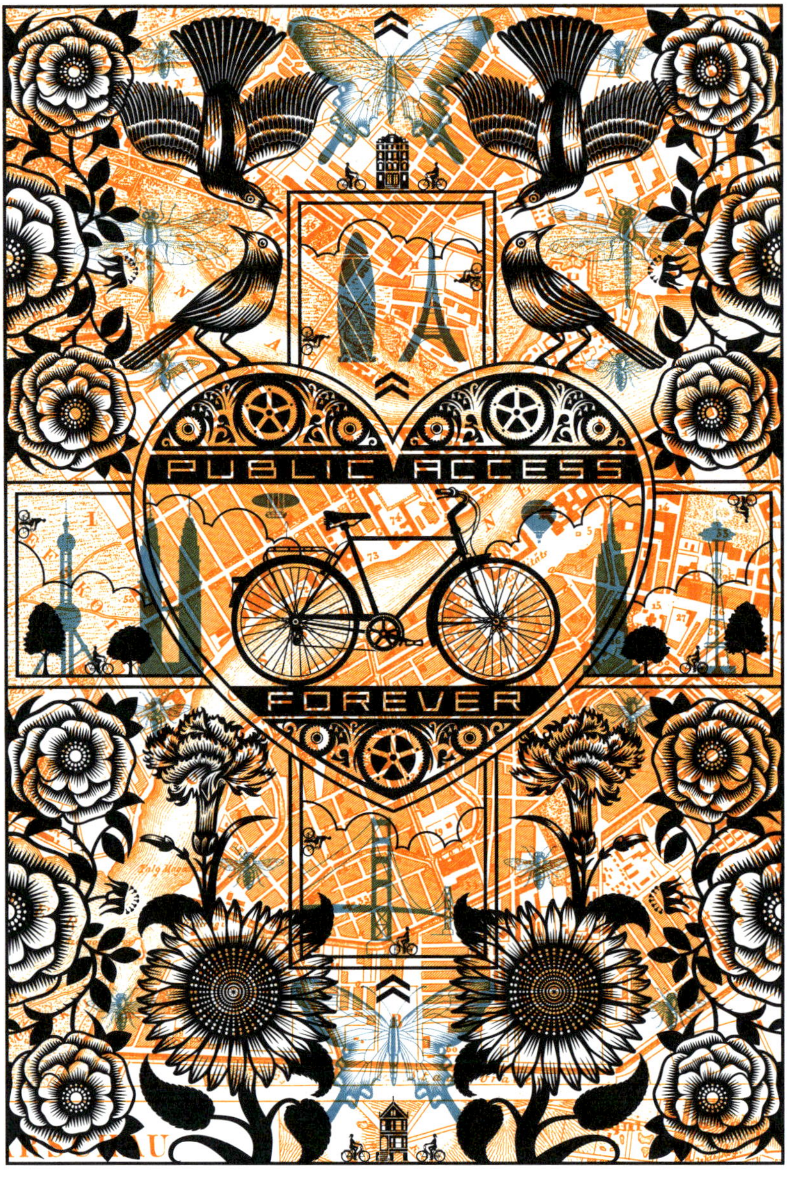

MICHAEL MABRY

Everyone has the right to walk
from one end of the city to the other in secure and
beautiful spaces. Everybody has the right
to go by public transport. Everybody has the right to an
unhampered view down their street, not full
of railings, signs and rubbish.

Richard Rogers

PUBLIC WORKS

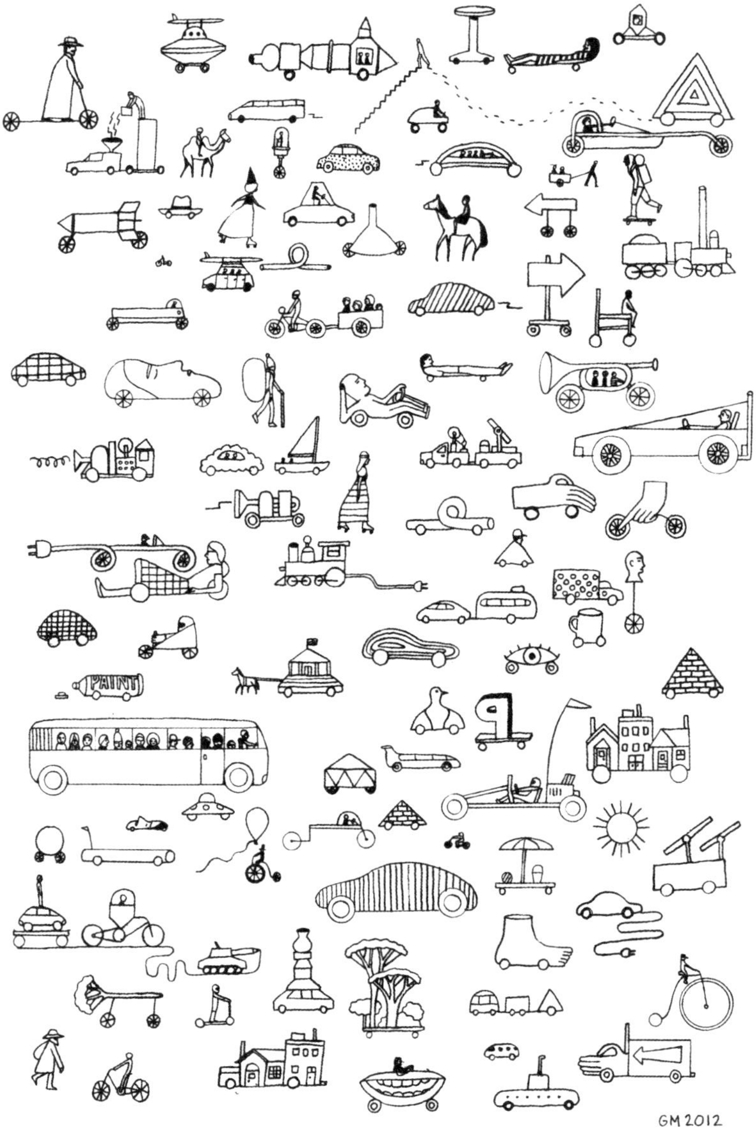

GEOFF MCFETRIDGE

As a kid I had a dream—
I wanted to own my own bicycle. When I got the bike
I must have been the happiest boy in Liverpool,
maybe the world. I lived for that bike. Most kids left their bike in
the backyard at night. Not me. I insisted on taking
mine indoors and the first night I even kept it in my bed.
John Lennon

PUBLIC WORKS

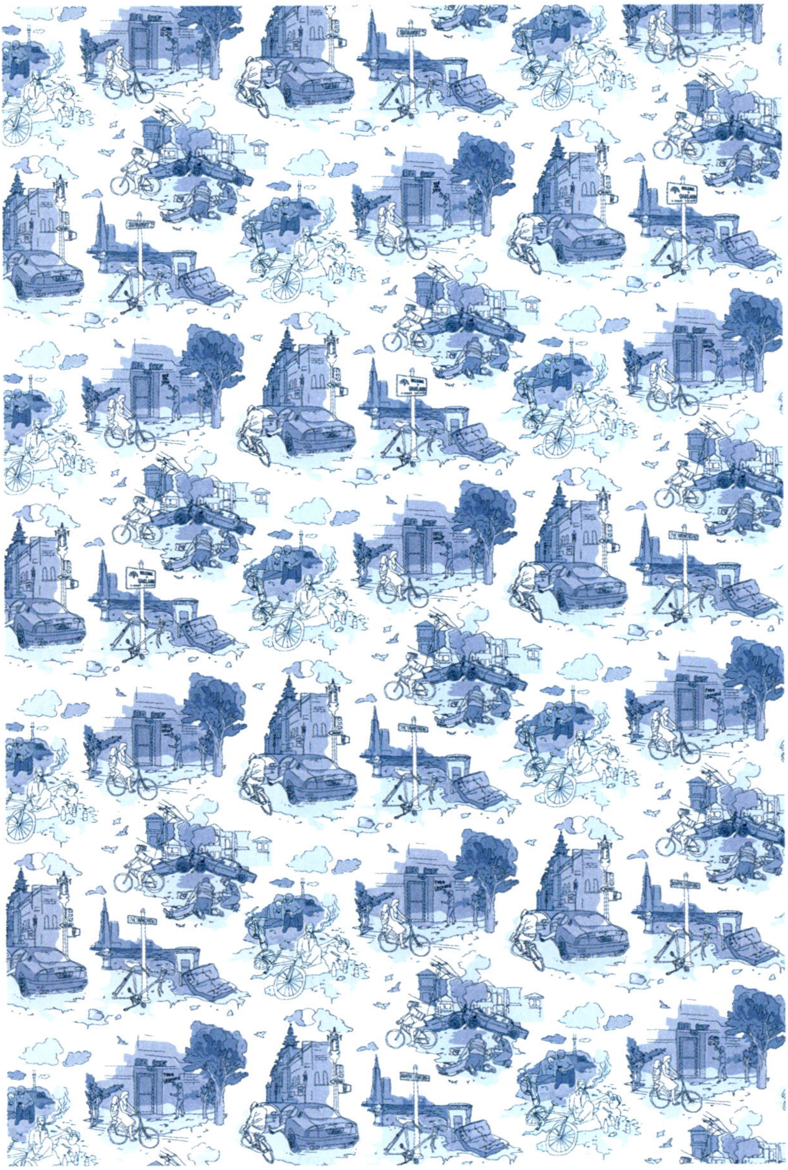

JEREMY MENDE

Place Matters:
The kind of environment you create for yourself
makes a real and tangible difference
in your level of happiness, health, and satisfaction.
Malcolm Gladwell

PUBLIC WORKS

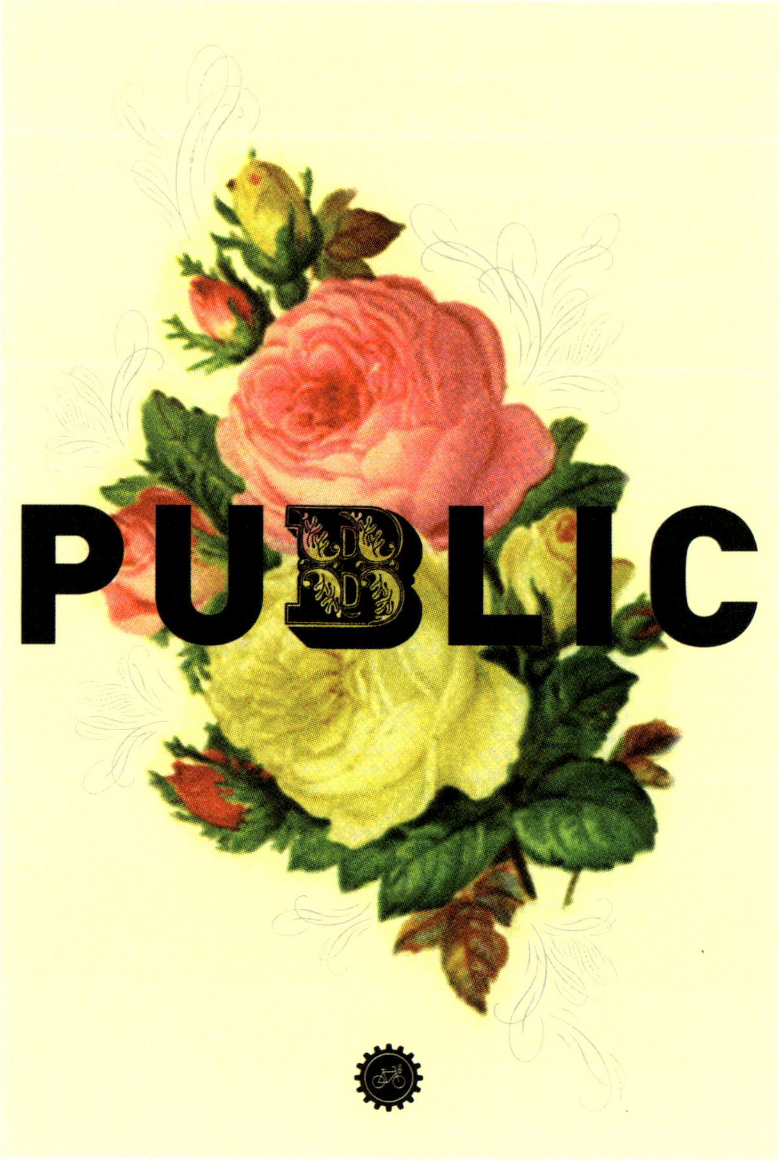

JENNIFER MORLA

When you take a flower in
your hand and really look at it, it's your world for
the moment. I want to give that world to
someone else. Most people in the city rush around so, they
have no time to look at a flower. I want them to
see it whether they want to or not.

Georgia O'Keefe

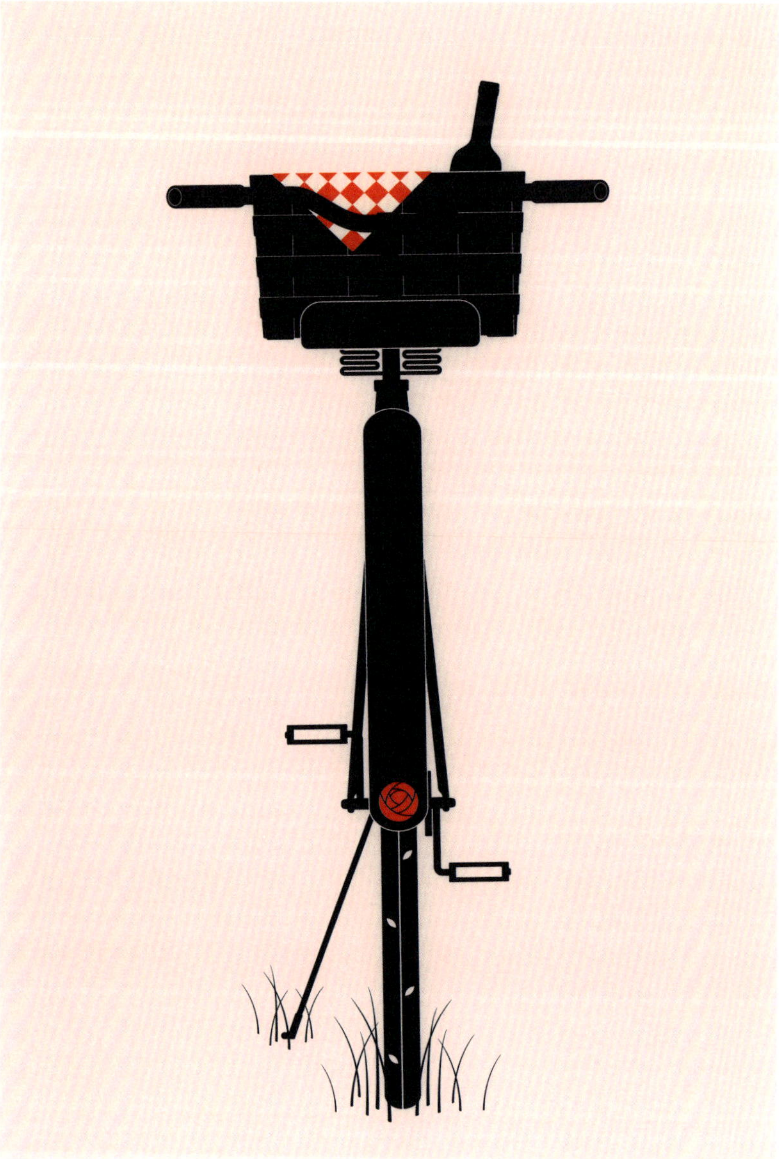

JASON MUNN

Things look different from
the seat of a bike carrying a sleeping bag with
a cold beer tucked on the inside.

Jim Malusa

PUBLIC WORKS

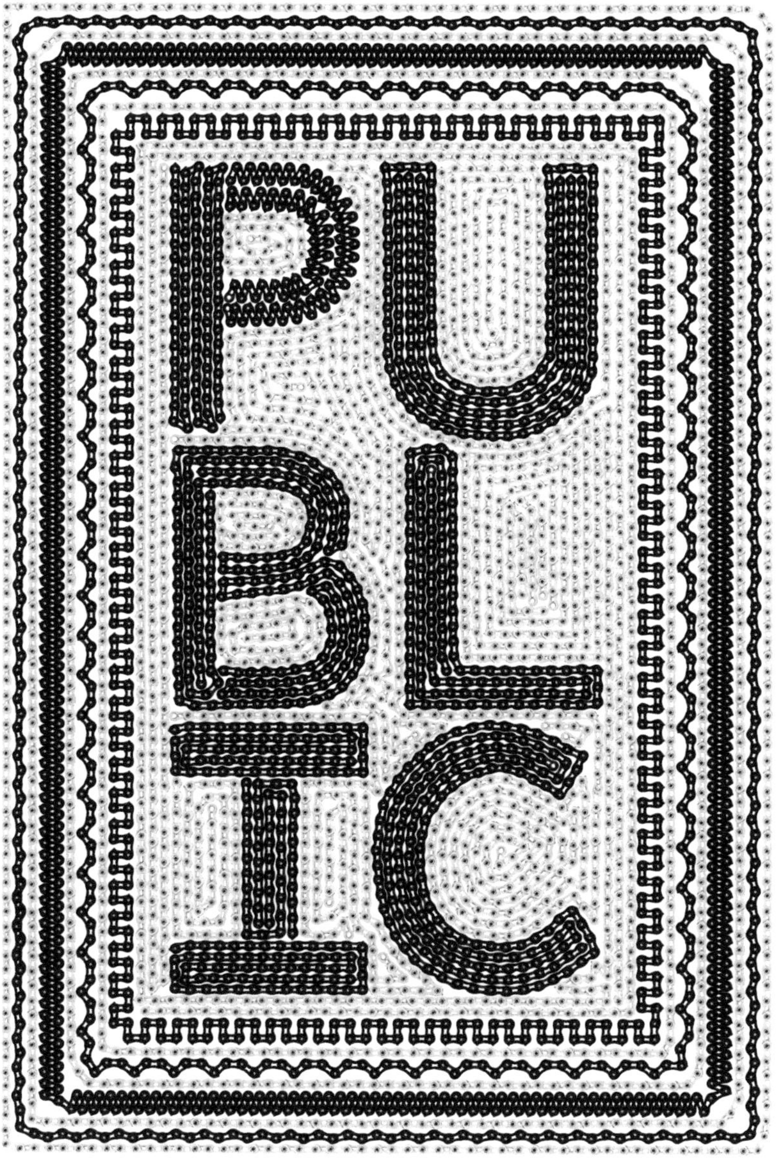

STEFAN SAGMEISTER & JESSICA WALSH

Our politicians talk sometimes
as if the only things we care about are private goods.
And they gloss over the fact that for many of us,
the most important things that can improve our lives are public
goods, the things that only can be bought collectively.
Malcolm Gladwell

PUBLIC WORKS

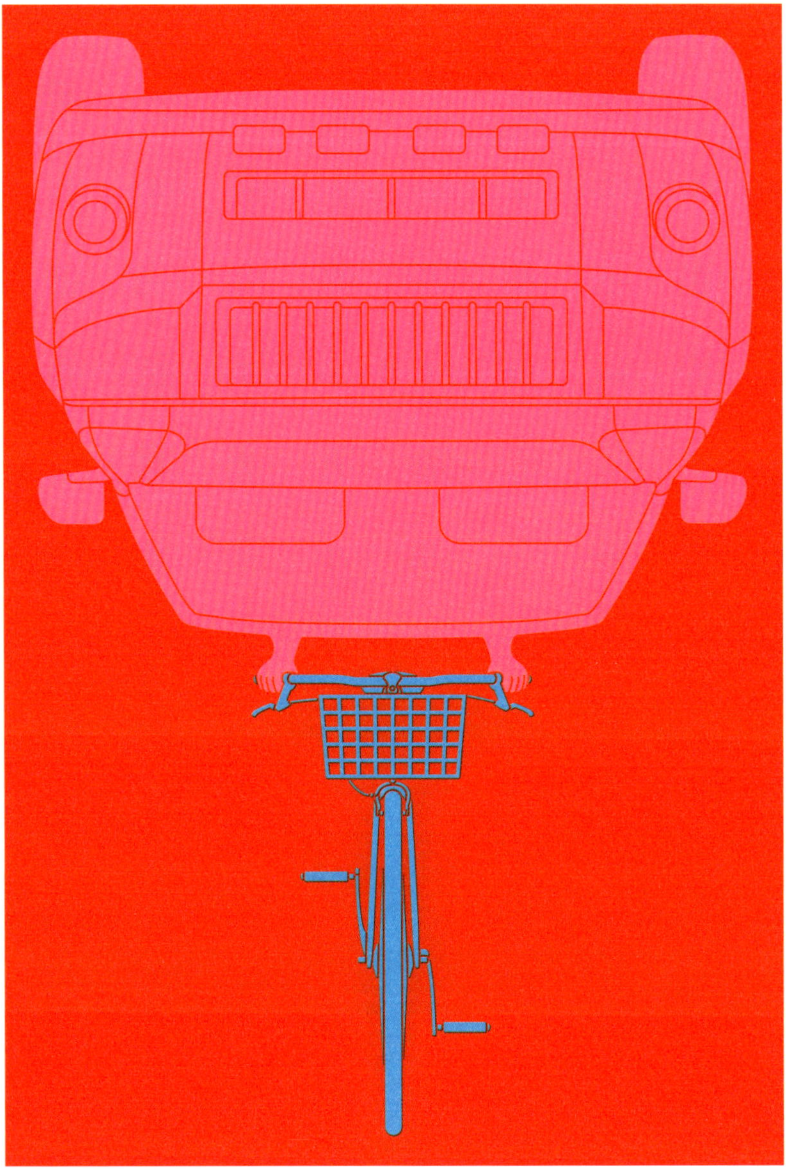

PAUL SAHRE

It is curious with the advent of the
automobile and the airplane, the bicycle is still with us.
Gurdon S. Leete

PUBLIC WORKS

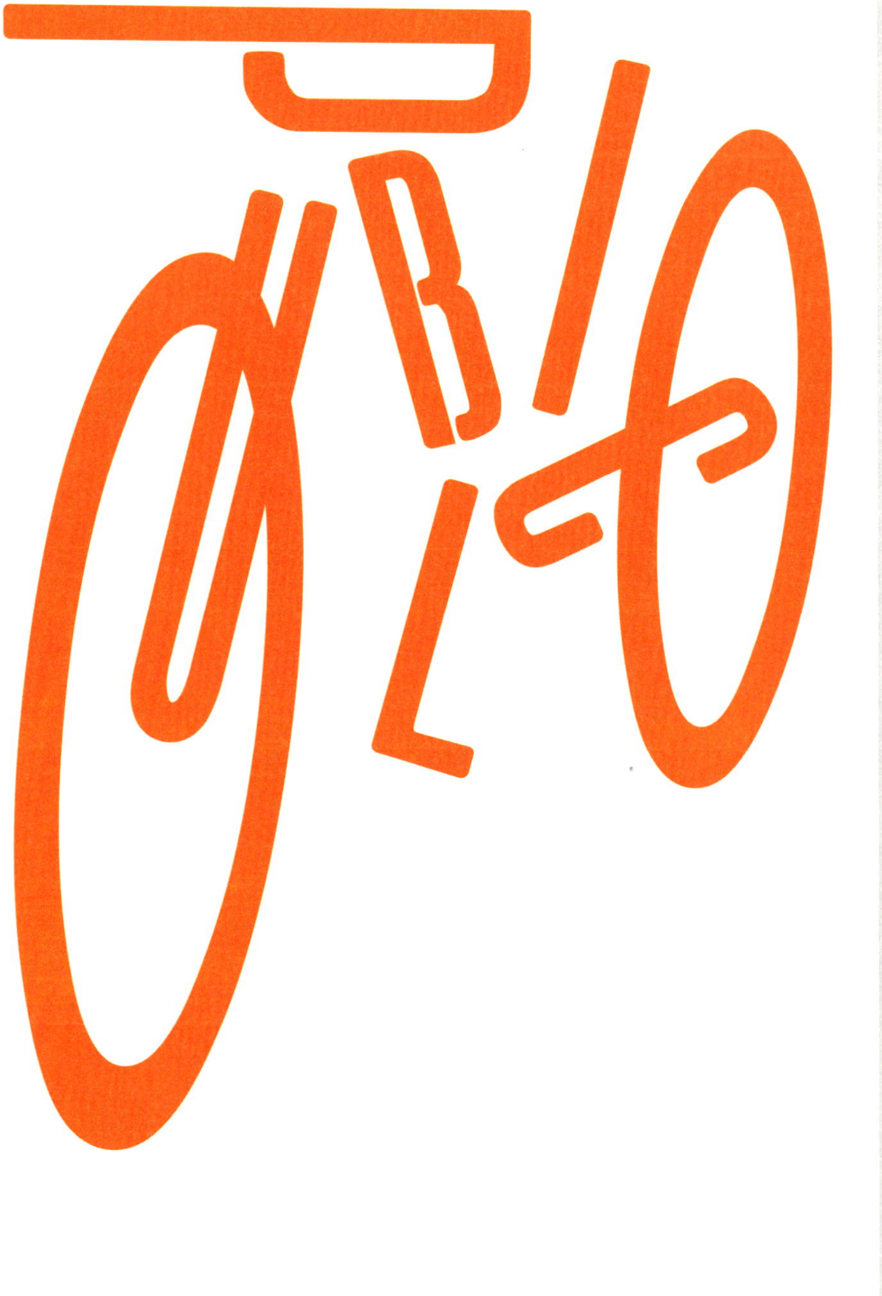

PAULA SCHER

(On the theory of relativity)
I thought of that while riding a bike
Albert Einstein

PUBLIC WORKS

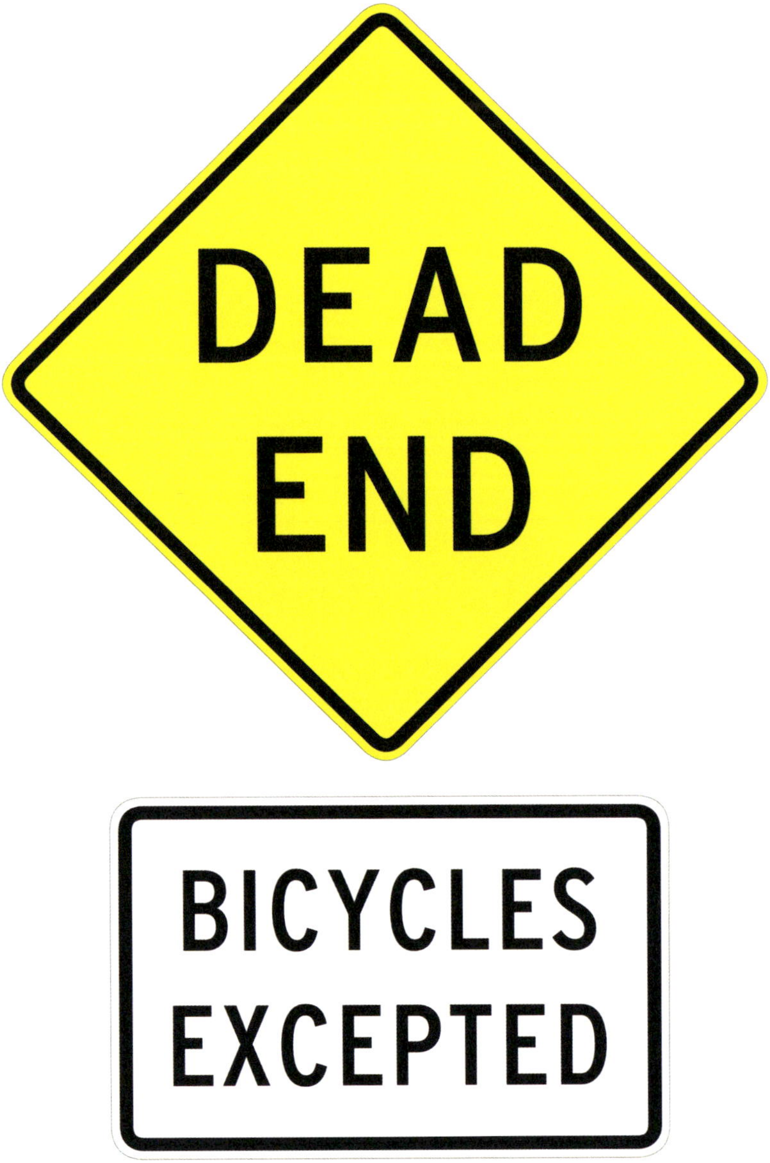

RALPH SCHRAIVOGEL

The bicycle is the most civilized conveyance
known to man. Others forms of transport grow daily more
nightmarish. Only the bicycle remains pure at heart.

Iris Murdoch

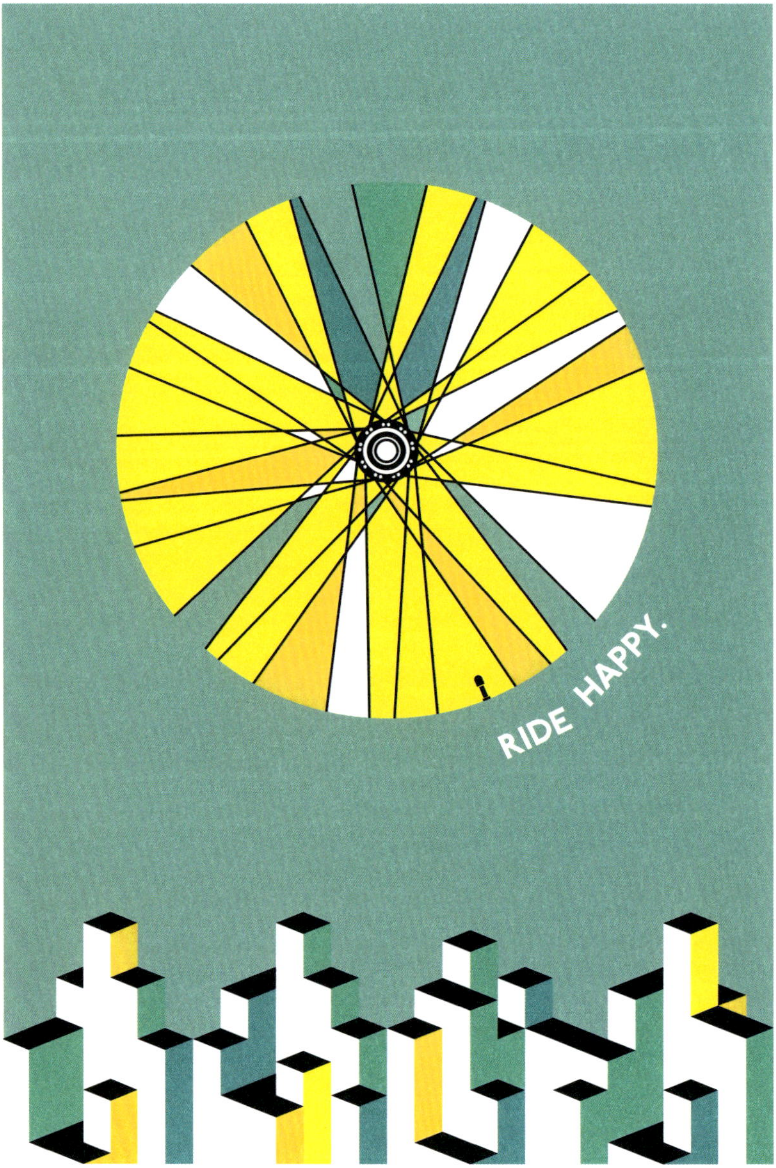

JASON SCHULTE

What suburbia cries for are the
means for people to gather easily, inexpensively, regularly,
and pleasurably—a 'place on the corner,' real
life alternatives to television, easy escapes from the cabin fever
of marriage and family life that do not necessitate
getting into an automobile.

Ray Oldenburg

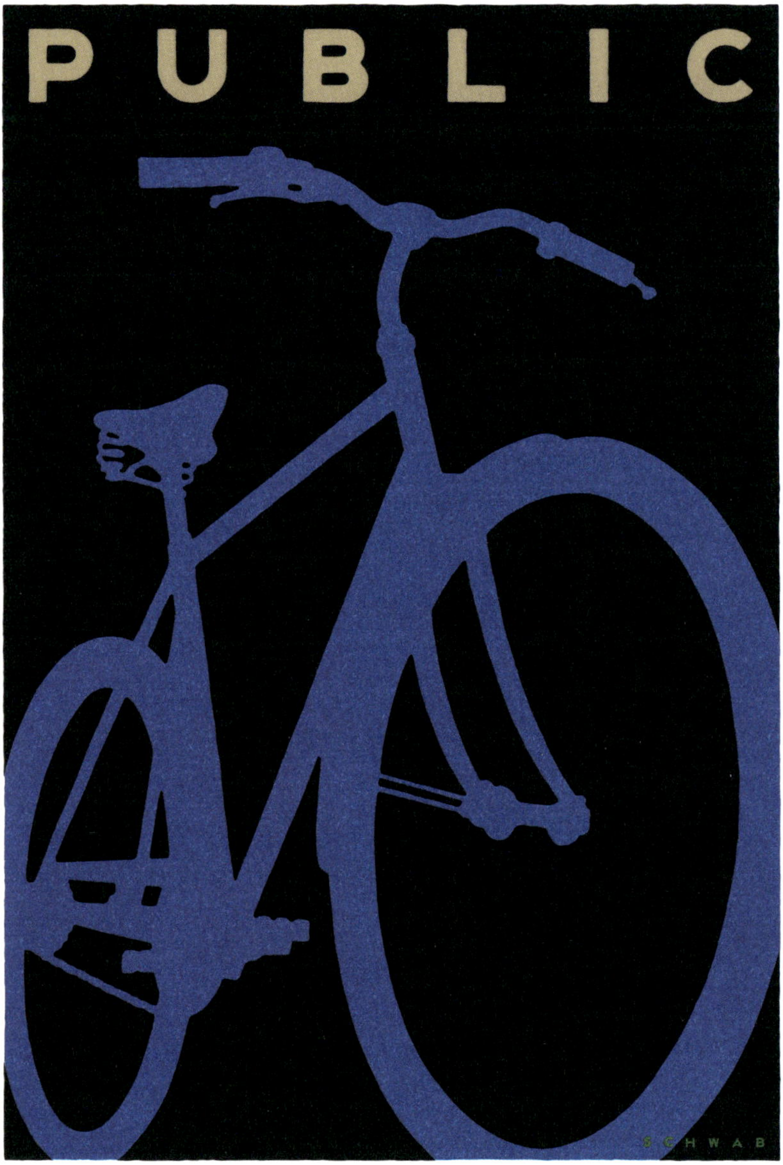

MICHAEL SCHWAB

Every time I see an adult on a bicycle,
I no longer despair for the future of the human race.

HG Wells

PUBLIC WORKS

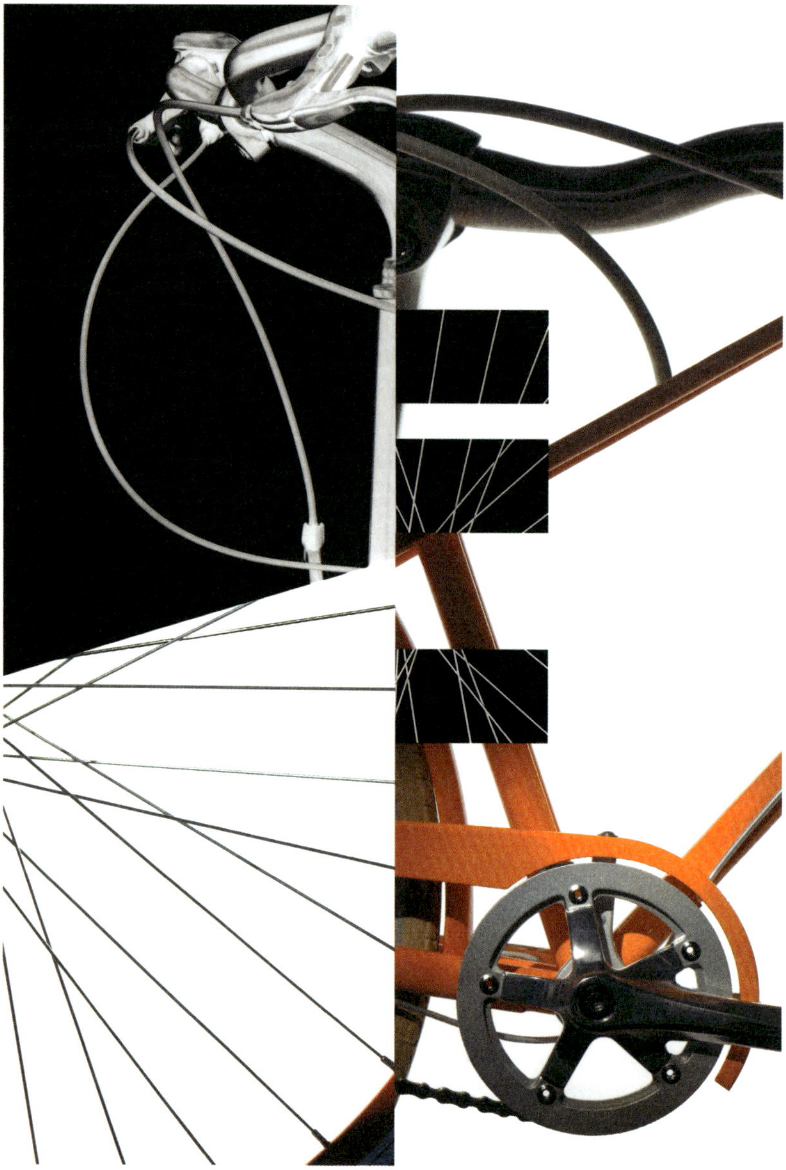

SKOLOS-WEDELL

Life is like riding a bicycle.
To keep your balance you must keep moving.
Albert Einstein

PUBLIC

space | enemy | park | toilet | radio
access | view | entrance | building
baths | company | enterprise | deal
transport | information | opinion
money | private partnership | pool
utility | relations | surplus | library
storage | gardens | passage | vote
performance | works | playground
announcement | school | crossing
grounds | beach | records | transit
housing | data | declaration | issue
parking | train | bicycles | persona
institution | address | appearance

ERIK SPIEKERMANN

Public sentiment is everything.
With public sentiment, nothing can fail.
Without it, nothing can succeed.
Abraham Lincoln

PUBLIC WORKS

JENNIFER STERLING

A city is a place where there is no need
to wait for next week to get the answer to a question,
to taste the food of any country, to find new
voices to listen to and familiar ones to listen to again.

Margaret Mead

PUBLIC WORKS

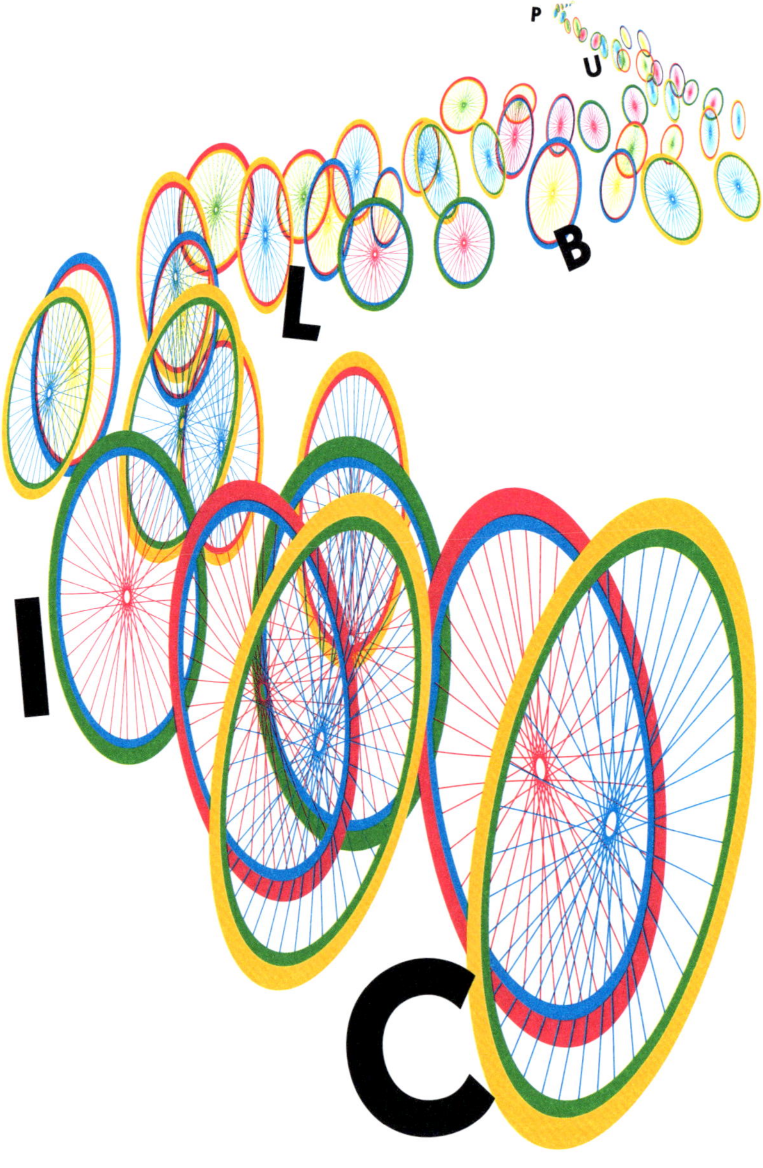

NIKLAUS TROXLER

It is by riding a bicycle that you
learn the contours of a country best, since you have to
sweat up the hills and coast down them.

Ernest Hemingway

PUBLIC WORKS

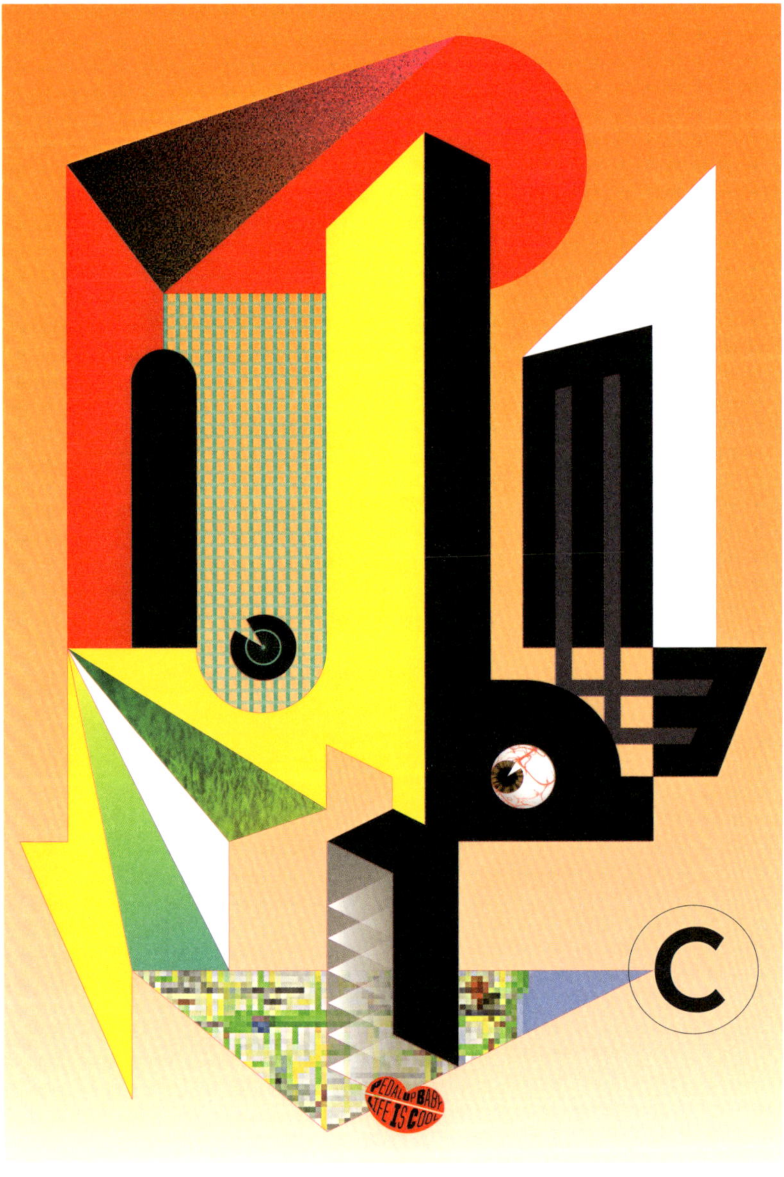

RICK VALICENTI

By its nature, the metropolis
provides what otherwise could be given only
by traveling; namely, the strange.

Jane Jacobs

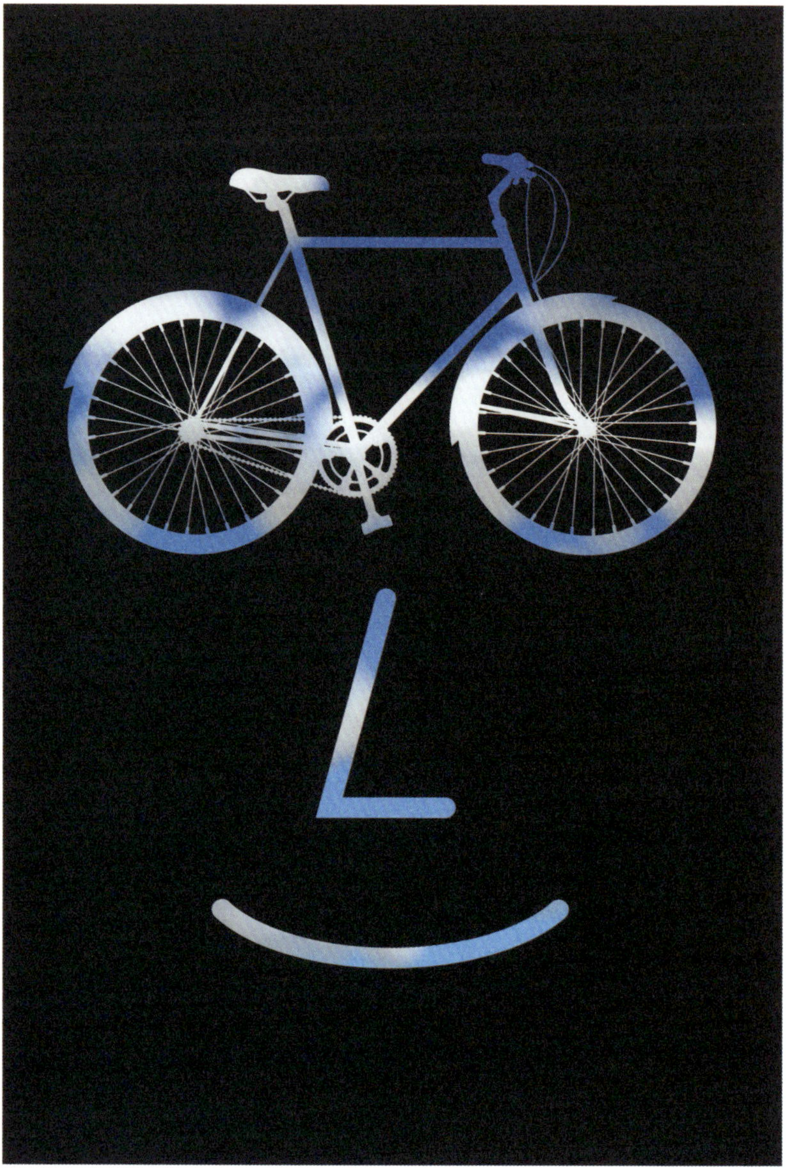

MICHAEL VANDERBYL

Get a bicycle. You will not regret it if you live.

Mark Twain

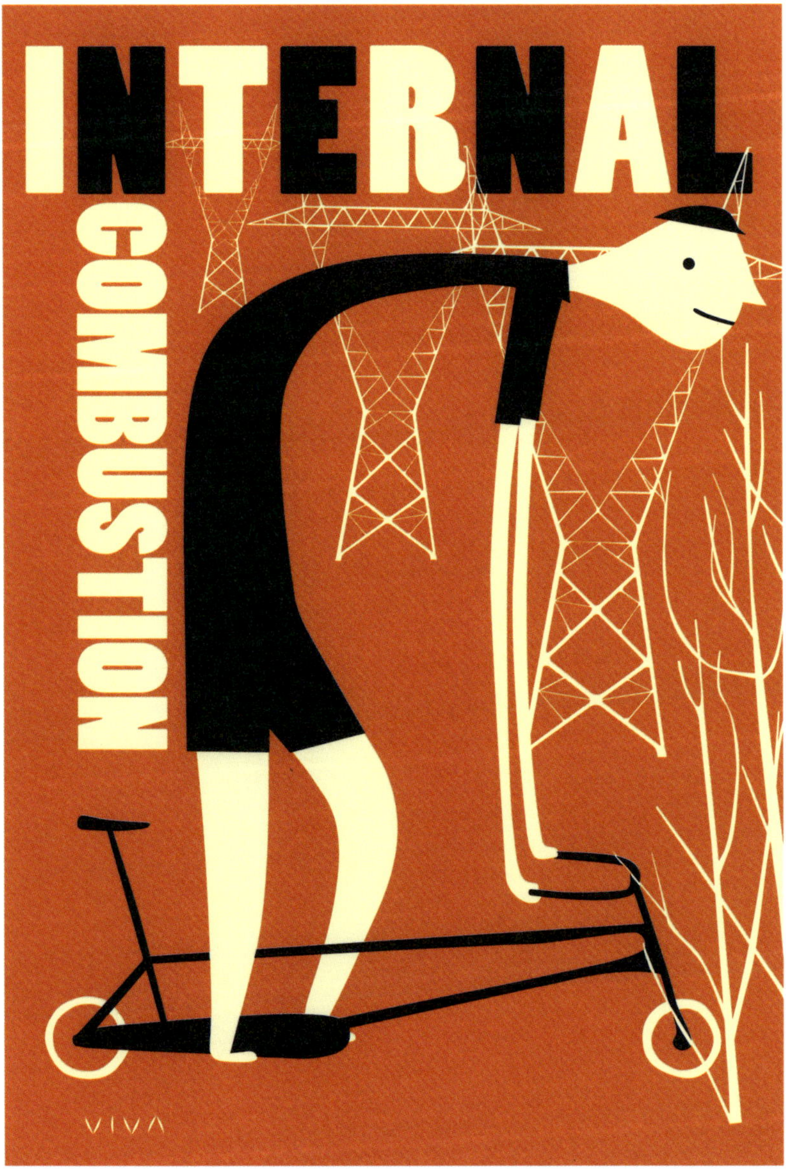
INTERNAL
COMBUSTION
VIVA

The bicycle is the most efficient
machine ever created. Converting calories into gas, a bicycle gets
the equivalent of three thousand miles per gallon.

Bill Strickland

PUBLIC WORKS

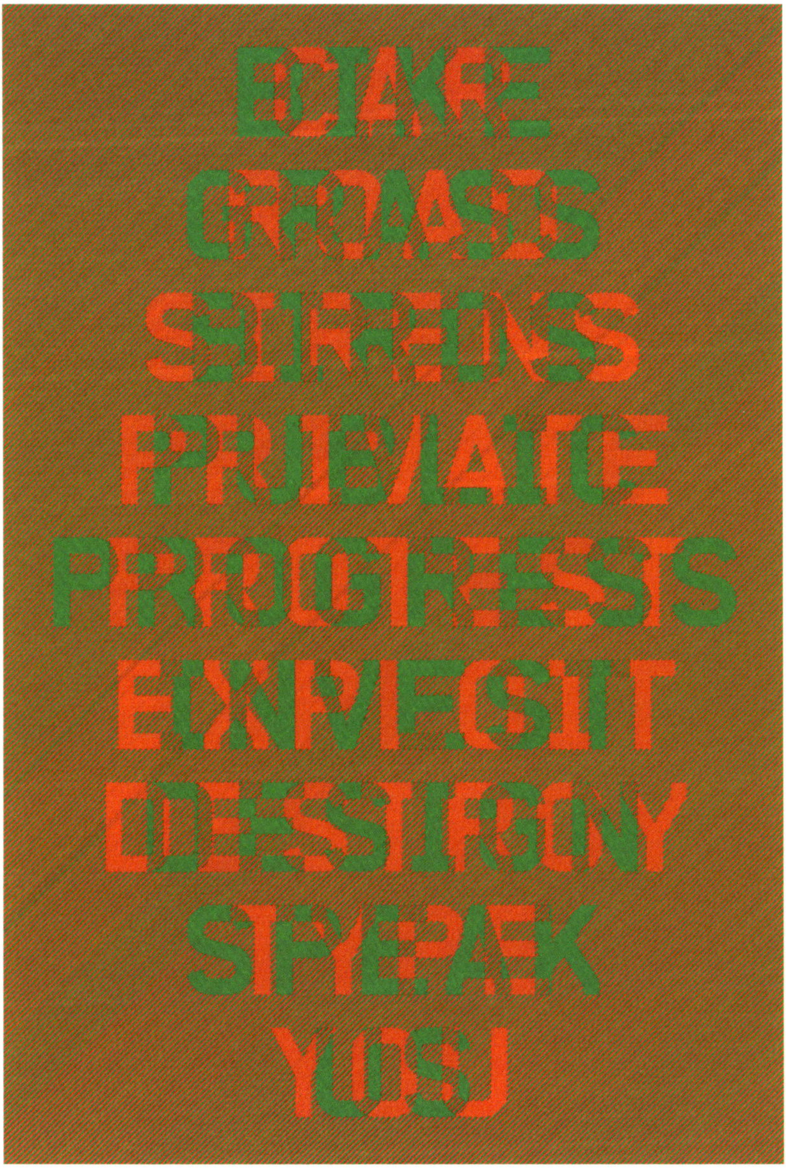

VOLUME INC.

Progress should have
stopped when man invented the bicycle.

Elizabeth West

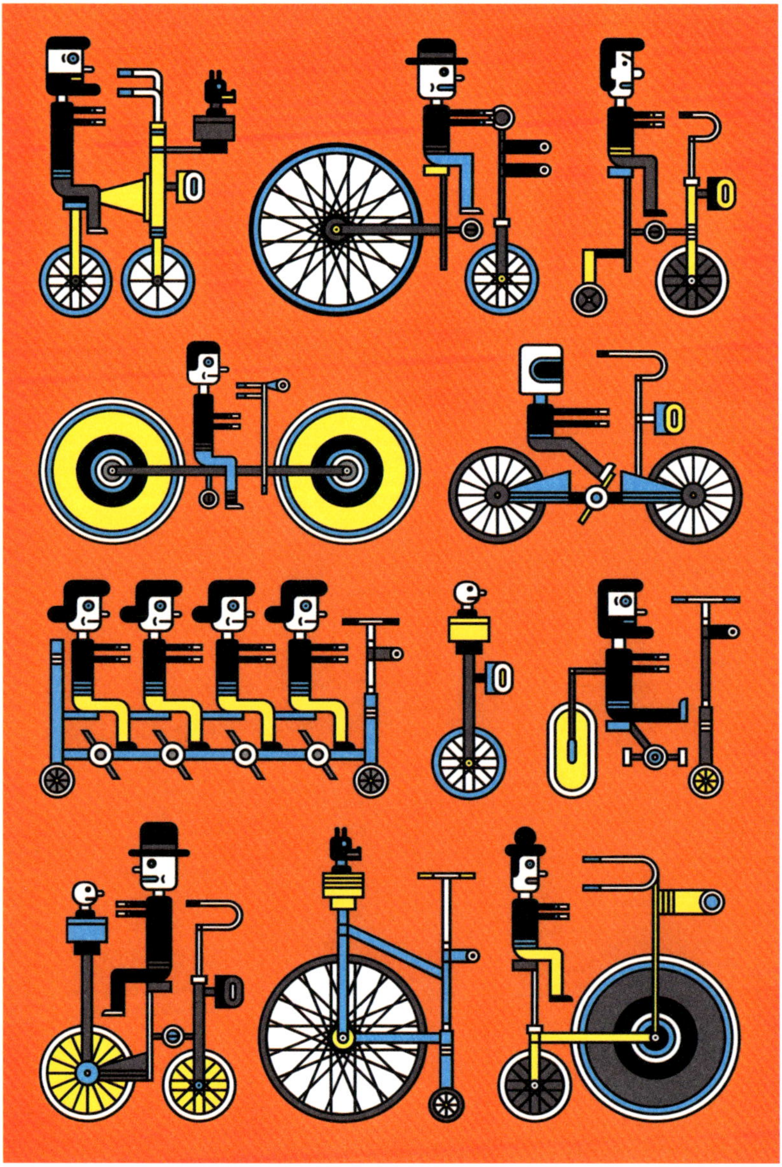

HENNING WAGENBRETH

The bicycle is a curious vehicle. Its passenger is its engine.

John Howard

THE ARTISTS

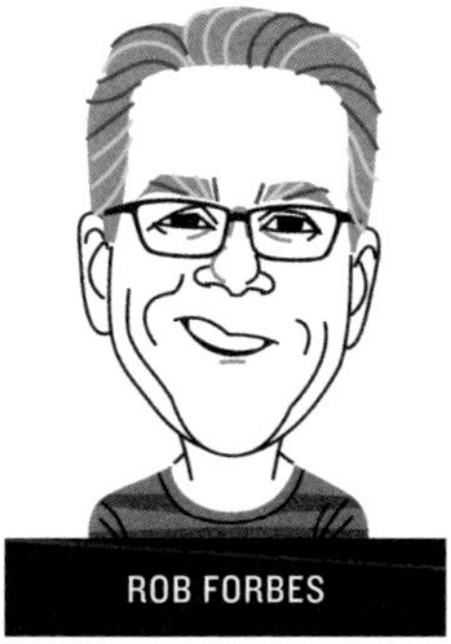

"WE INVITED THIS PRESTIGIOUS AND DIVERSE GROUP OF INTERNATIONAL ARTISTS, ILLUSTRATORS AND DESIGNERS TO HELP US BRING ATTENTION TO THE IMPORTANT ISSUES IN OUR PUBLIC WORLD. WE THANK THE CONTRIBUTORS FOR THEIR INSPIRATIONAL AND UNIQUE WORKS."

– ROB FORBES, PUBLIC

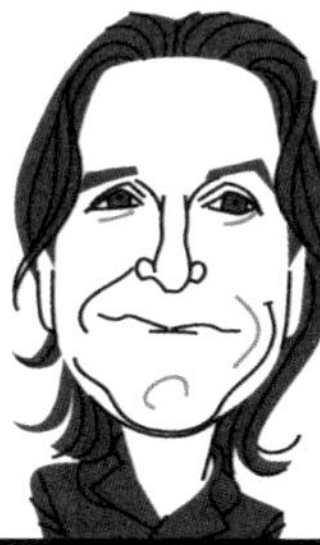

DANA ARNETT

Dana Arnett is a founding Principal and CEO of the internationally recognized firm VSA Partners headquartered in Chicago. The firm designs programs, digital and interactive initiatives and brand marketing solutions. VSA Partners' diverse client roster includes: Harley-Davidson, IBM, General Electric, Coca-Cola, Thomson Reuters and Nike. Dana is also active as an advisor and member of the business development and capital group, Cueball Collective that helps fund and incubate consumer and socially driven ventures.

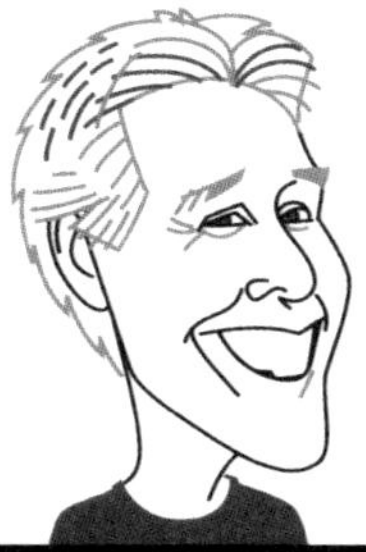

JOHN BIELENBERG

John Bielenberg is a co-founder of FUTURE, a San Francisco based design group that takes a radical humanitarian approach to problem solving. Bielenberg also founded Project M, a program designed to inspire and educate young designers, writers, photographers, and filmmakers by proving that design can have a positive and significant impact on the world.

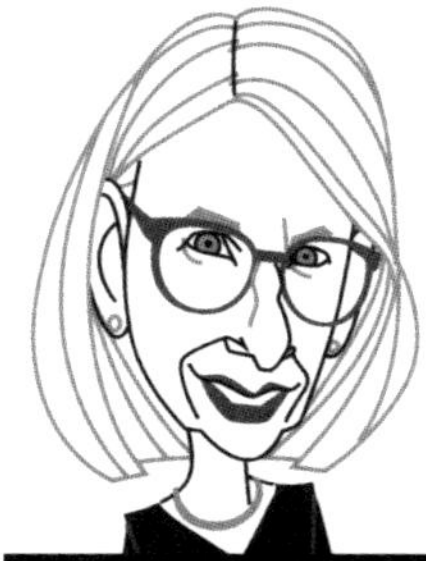

ROZ CHAST

Roz Chast, a well-known illustrator, began contributing to The New Yorker in 1978. Since then she has contributed over 1,000 cartoons and nine covers to the magazine. She has also illustrated several children's books, most notably with the humor writer Patricia Marx and the actor Steve Martin. In April of 2012, she was one of six NYC Literary Honorees and received the Humor award from Mayor Bloomberg.

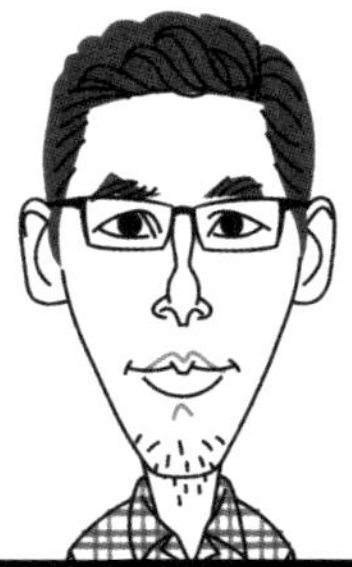

FRANK CHIMERO

Frank Chimero, a Brooklyn-based graphic designer and illustrator, often uses symbolism, concepts, and storytelling to create thought provoking pieces. His clients include The New York Times, Nike, Wired, Microsoft, Bloomberg-Business Week, Newsweek, The Atlantic, Starbucks, GOOD and others. Frank's work has appeared on both The Colbert Report and The Suite Life with Zach and Cody, spanning the full quality-spectrum of television.

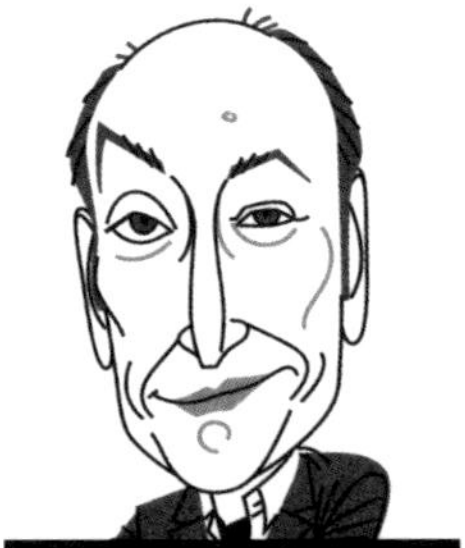

MILTON GLASER

New York based Milton Glaser co-founded the revolutionary Pushpin Studios in 1954, founded New York Magazine with Clay Felker in 1968, and established Milton Glaser, Inc. in 1974. Throughout his career Glaser has been a prolific creator of posters and prints — many of which have become iconic. Glaser's contribution to cities and design is best appreciated through his I Heart NY logo done in 1976.

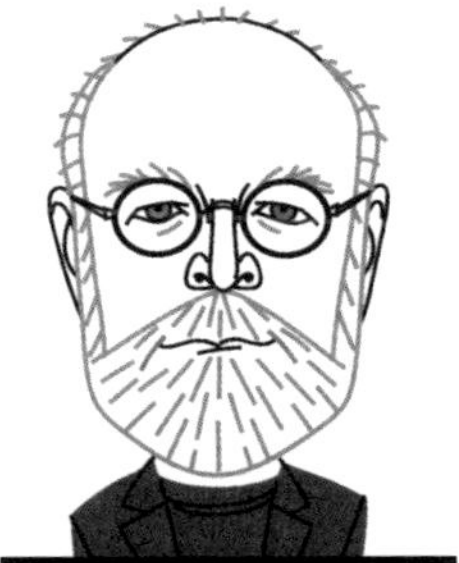

KIT HINRICHS

Kit Hinrichs founded San Francisco based Studio Hinrichs following a 23 year career as a partner in Pentagram Design. His work is characterized by its narrative quality and an encyclopedic set of cultural references. His instincts as a visual storyteller and a collector influence his work. His 5,000-piece-strong collection of American flags and American flag memorabilia has formed the basis of several exhibitions and two books. He is also an AIGA medalist and is included in MOMA's permanent collection.

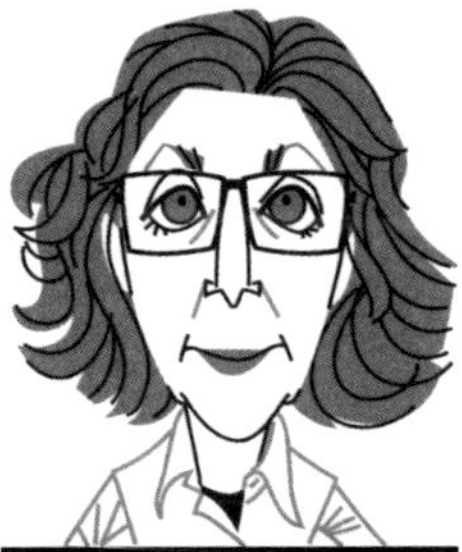

MAIRA KALMAN

Maira Kalman, a well-known writer and illustrator, has published over thirteen children's books, contributes frequently to The New Yorker and has been featured in The New York Times, Newsweek, Interview, and many other publications. Her columns for the New York Times were collected in book form and published by Penguin Press. Kalman has also designed products for the Museum of Modern Art under the M&Co. label, fabric for Isaac Mizrahi, accessories for Kate Spade, and sets for Mark Morris Dance Group.

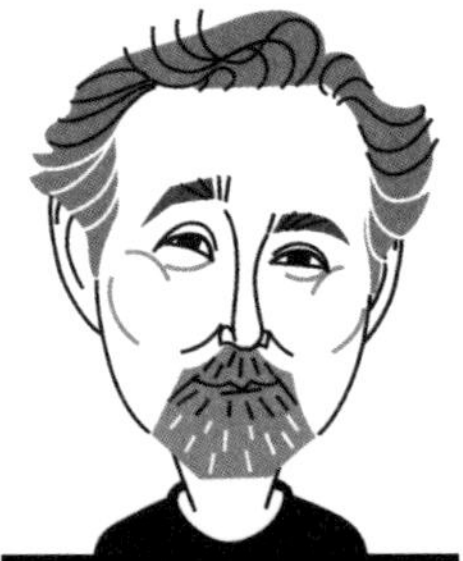

MICHAEL MABRY

Michael Mabry started his career as a senior designer for Nicolas Sidjakov and Jerry Berman at SBG Partners in San Francisco. In 1981, he opened his own studio. Throughout his career, Michael has created distinctive brand and corporate identities, packaging systems and illustrations for a variety of individualistic companies, including Chronicle Books, Hewlett Packard Corporation, The Land of Nod, Lucas Films, The Mellon Foundation, Martha Stewart Omnimedia, Netjets Europe, The New York Times, and The Oakland Museum of California.

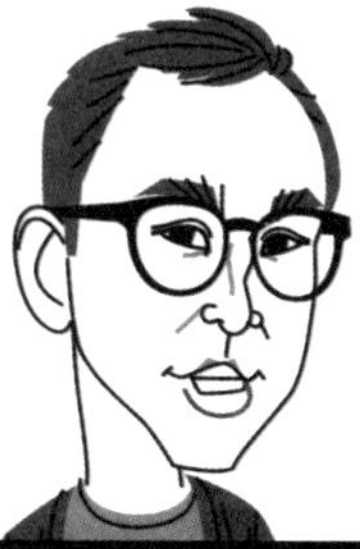

GEOFF MCFETRIDGE

Los Angeles based Geoff McFetridge, founder of Champion Graphics, is known for his reductive graphic style. He was part of the Beautiful Losers: Contemporary Art and Street Culture exhibition that toured the world, and has made solo exhibitions in Los Angeles, New York, Berlin, Paris, London, Seattle, Milan and the Netherlands. His clients include Nike, Patagonia, Vans, MTV, Pepsi, and The New York Times.

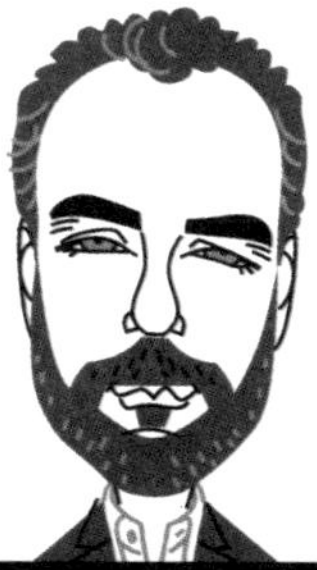

JEREMY MENDE

Jeremy Mende is a visual designer from San Francisco, California. In 2000 he founded Mende Design, a creative firm that balances commercial projects with visual research and public art. His work defines design as equal parts expression, criticism, intuition, and advocacy. Mende is an Associate Professor of Design and Graphic Design at the California College of the Arts.

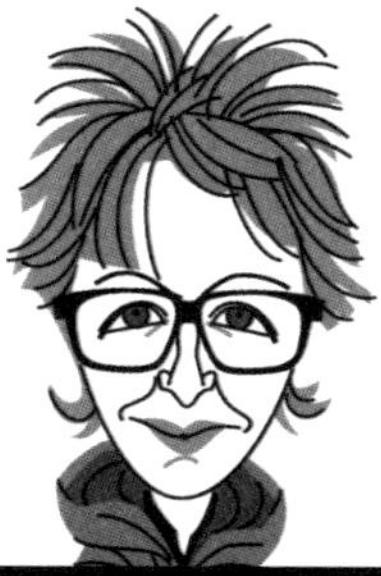

JENNIFER MORLA

Jennifer Morla, President and Creative Director of Morla Design, San Francisco has been recognized by virtually every organization in the field of visual communication. Since opening Morla Design in 1984, she has continued to pair wit and elegance on everything from motion graphics and branding to retail environments and textiles. Morla's work is part of the permanent collections of many museums including MoMA and SFMoMA, the Smithsonian Museum, the Denver Art Museum, and the Library of Congress.

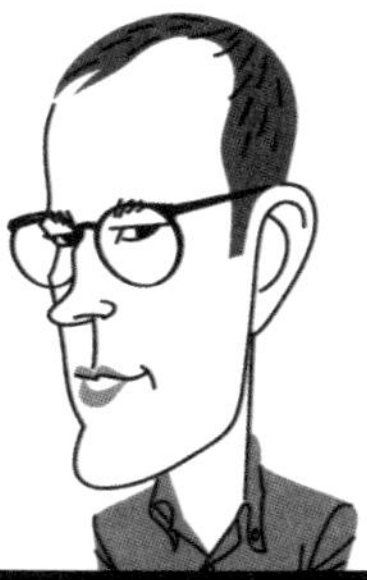

JASON MUNN

Jason Munn's career started under the pseudonym The Small Stakes designing posters for local venues and independent musicians in the San Francisco Bay Area. Now working under his name, Munn continues to focus on posters, as well as design and illustration commissions. His work has appeared in numerous exhibits and publications. Munn's clients include San Francisco Museum of Modern Art, Chronicle Books, Noise Pop Festival, Patagonia, Death Cab for Cutie, Flight Of The Conchords, The National and many other well known bands.

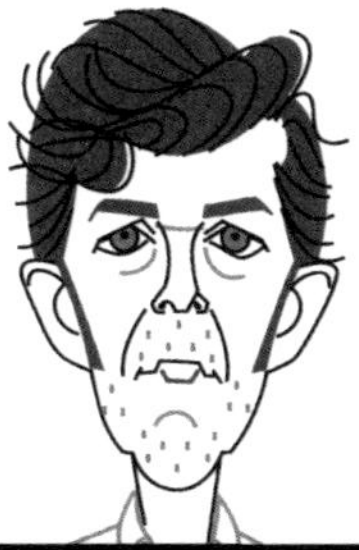

STEFAN SAGMEISTER

Stefan Sagmeister was born in Austria and lives and works in New York. He has worked for the Rolling Stones, The Talking Heads, Lou Reed, The Guggenheim Museum and Levis. Exhibitions on Sagmeister's work have been mounted in New York, Philadelphia, Tokyo, Osaka, Seoul, Paris, Lausanne, Zurich, Vienna, Prague, Cologne and Berlin.

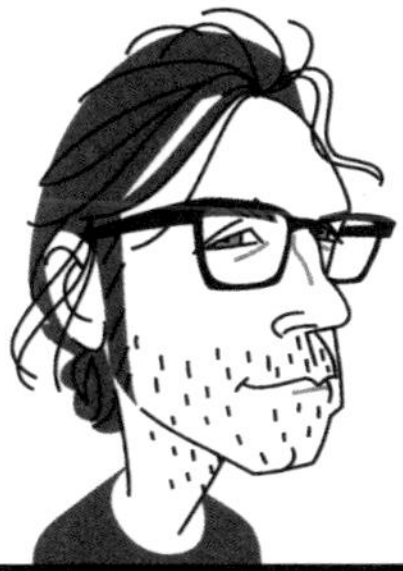

PAUL SAHRE

Paul Sahre works across multiple disciplines as a graphic designer, illustrator, lecturer, educator and author. Sahre established his New York studio in 1997. Notable for the design of books and book covers for authors such as Malcolm Gladwell, Rick Moody, Chuck Klosterman, Ben Marcus and Ernest Hemingway. Sahre is also a frequent visual contributor to The New York Times.

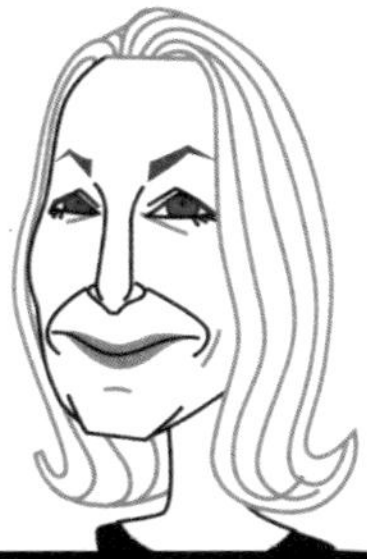

PAULA SCHER

Paula Scher began her career as a record cover art director at both Atlantic and CBS Records in the 1970s. In 1991 she joined Pentagram as a partner. She has developed identity and branding systems, promotional materials, environmental graphics, packaging and publication designs for a wide range of clients. Her work has been exhibited worldwide and is in the permanent collections of the Museum of Modern Art, the Cooper-Hewitt National Design Museum, and the Centre Georges Pompidou.

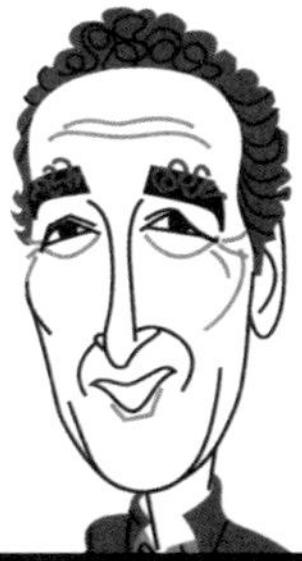

RALPH SCHRAIVOGEL

Ralph Schraivogel opened his own graphic design studio in Zurich in 1982. He designs publications, logos and corporate identities, but devotes himself to creating posters for cultural events. He has designed posters and program magazines for the Zurich repertory cinema "Filmpodium" since 1983. He has repeatedly been commissioned to design posters and exhibit announcements for the Museum für Gestaltung Zürich since 1984.

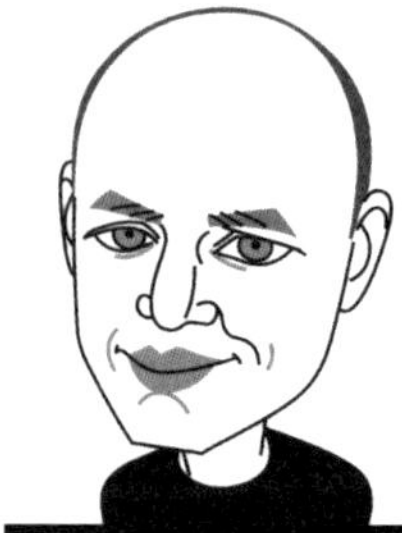

JASON SCHULTE

San Francisco based Jason Schulte founded Office, a creative studio that crafts strategies and designs experiences to make things better. Since founding Office in 2003, Jason Schulte has led differentiated solutions for some of the world's most iconic companies, including Coca-Cola, Google, Apple, Target, Disney, eBay, and Carlsberg.

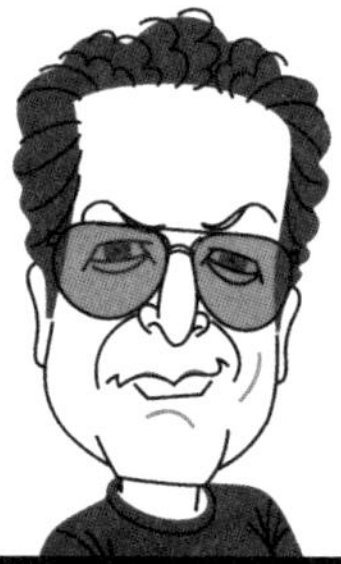

MICHAEL SCHWAB

San Francisco Bay Area based Michael Schwab focuses on the interplay of positive and negative space to create his signature graphic style, including several iconic American posters and logos. His clients include Amtrak, the National Park Service, Major League Baseball, Muhammad Ali, Pebble Beach, Robert Redford and the San Francisco Opera and America's Cup. His work resides in the permanent collections of the San Francisco Museum of Modern Art, the California Palace of the Legion of Honor and the National Portrait Gallery in Washington, DC.

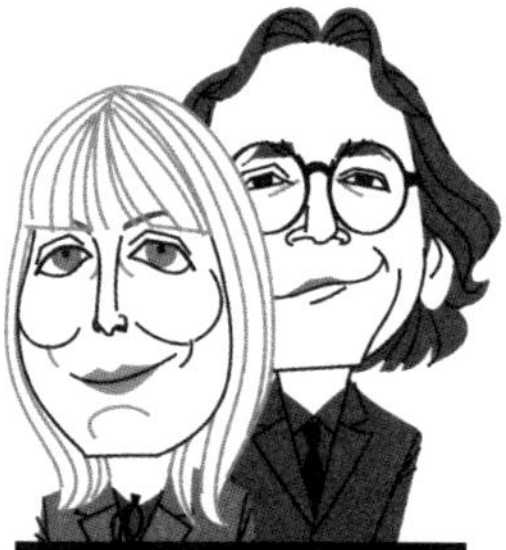

SKOLOS - WEDELL

Massachusetts based Nancy Skolos and Thomas Wedell work to diminish the boundaries between graphic design and photography—creating collaged three-dimensional images influenced by modern painting, technology and architecture. Clients include Boston Acoustics, Callaway Editions, Cambridge Arts Council, EMI Music Publishing, Harvard Medical School, US Department of Health and Human Services, IDSA, Maine Lakes Conservancy, Rhode Island School of Design, Steelcase Design Partnership and the US Postal Service.

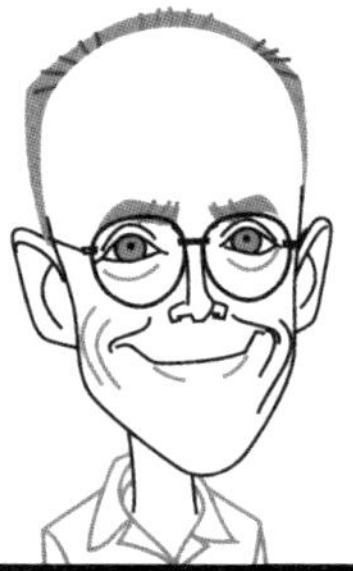

ERIK SPIEKERMANN

Berlin and San Francisco based Erik Spiekermann, managing partner of Edenspiekermann, is an information architect, type designer and author of books and articles on type and typography. Two of his typefaces, FF Meta and ITC Officina, are considered to be modern classics. He is behind the design of well-know brands such as Audi, Bosch, VW, German Railways and Heidelberg Printing, among others; information systems for Berlin Transit and Düsseldorf Airport and publications like The Economist.

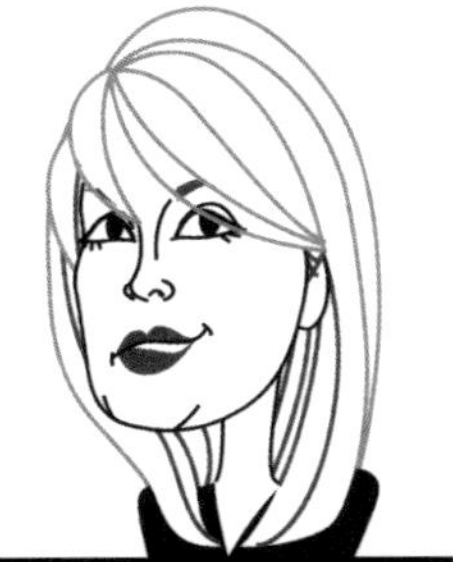

JENNIFER STERLING

Jennifer Sterling is a Graphic Designer, Artist, and Typographer based in New York. In 2000 Jennifer was inducted into Alliance Graphique Internationale as well as Who's Who in America. Add tionally she has served on the Design and Architecture Accessions Board of the SFMOMA. Her work resides in the permanent collections of the San Francisco Museum of Modern Art, Bibliothèque Nationale de France, Museum fur Kunst und Gewerbe Hamburg, The Cooper-Hewitt National Design Museum and The Library of Congress.

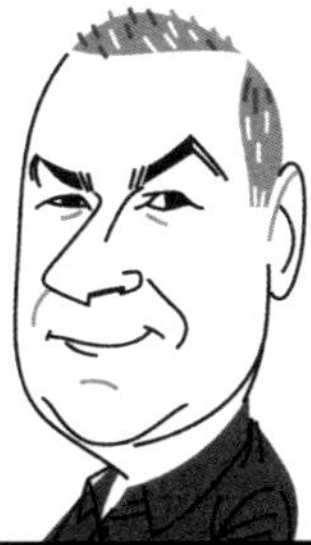

NICKLAUS TROXLER

In 1973 Niklaus Troxler founded his own studio in Willisau, Switzerland. He has organized and designed posters for jazz concerts since 1966 and an annual Jazz Festival from 1975 to 2009 in his hometown Willisau. He produces posters, CD and book covers, illustrations, typography, and designs for textiles, products, art and architecture. His work has been featured in New York, Minneapolis, Mexico, Buenos Aires, Caracas, Paris, Berlin, Warsaw, Tokyo, Beijing and Hangzhou.

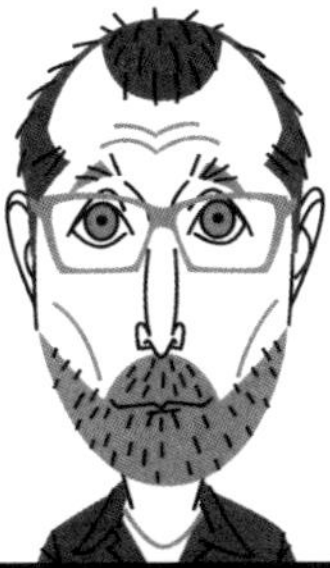

RICK VALICENTI

Rick Valicenti is the Founder and Design Director of Thirst, a communication design firm devoted to art, function and real human presence. He has been recognized for excellence in Communication Design for the Cooper-Hewitt, National Design Museum's 2011 National Design Awards program. Thirst's works are included in the permanent collections of the Cooper-Hewitt National Design Museum, the Museum of Modern Art, and the Art Institute of Chicago. Clients include AIGA, Harvard, Herman Miller, ESPN, and The New York Times.

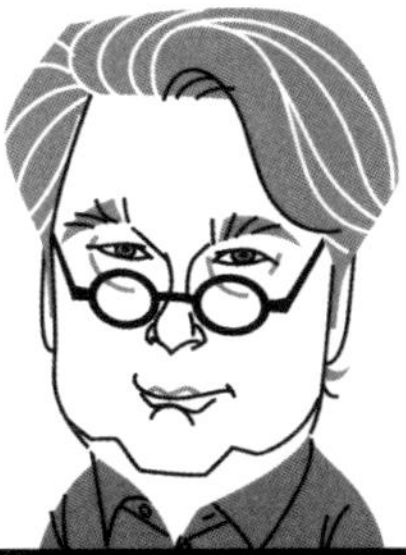

MICHAEL VANDERBYL

San Francisco Bay Area based Michael Vanderbyl, founded of Vanderbyl Design, a multidisciplinary studio with expertise in identity, print and digital communications, interiors, showrooms, retail spaces, signage, textiles, fashion apparel, packaging, furniture and product design. His work is included in the permanent collections of several museums and featured in national and international publications. Currently he presides as Dean of Design at the California College of the Arts. Clients include AIGA, Mohawk Fine Paper Inc., and Teknion Furniture Systems.

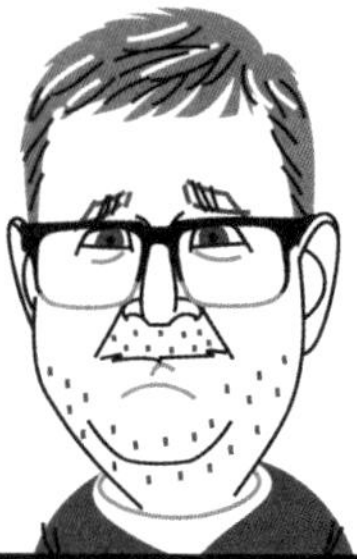

FRANK VIVA

Frank Viva is the founder and creative director of Toronto based Viva & Co. – a branding and design agency. In addition to being a frequent cover artist for The New Yorker, his clients include Le Creuset, Krups, All Clad, Butterfield & Robinson, and The New York Public Library. He is also a co-founder of Whigby, a small stationery company that designs and produces greeting cards, posters and other products that can be found at the MoMA store, Paul Smith and many other places.

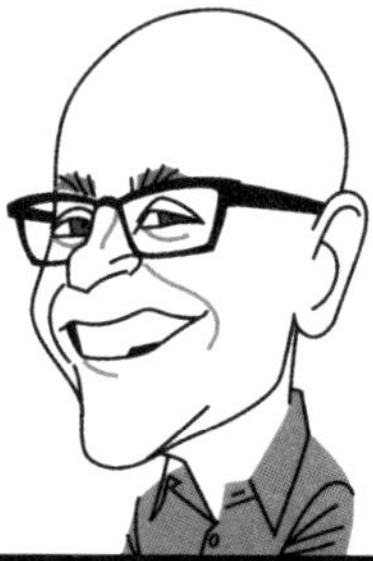

VOLUME INC.

Volume Inc. is the brainchild of Adam Brodsley and Eric Heiman, who have been creating compelling work of varying media, size, color, speed, and purpose for the last decade. Clients include California Academy of Sciences, Adobe Systems, San Francisco Museum of Modern Art (SFMOMA), Rizzoli, Yerba Buena Center for the Arts, Mohawk Fine Papers, Heath Ceramics, ReadyMade magazine, McSweeneys and 826 Valencia.

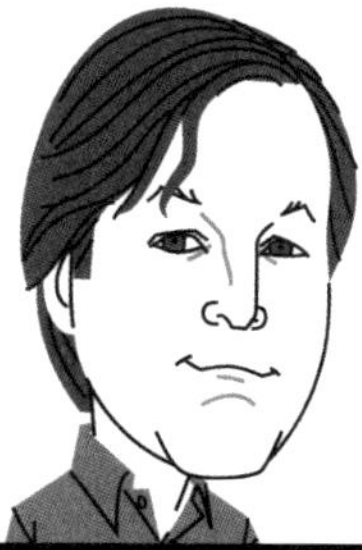

HENNING WAGENBRETH

German based Henning Wagenbreth focuses on illustration with a strong interest in graphics and typography. He possesses a strong understanding of manual and industrial printing techniques, as he believes they are an essential part of the creative process. Internationally recognized for his unique, comic inspired style that has been featured on many posters, books and magazines. His artwork can be found on anything from a tiny stamp to an oversized poster, on commercial work or free art projects.

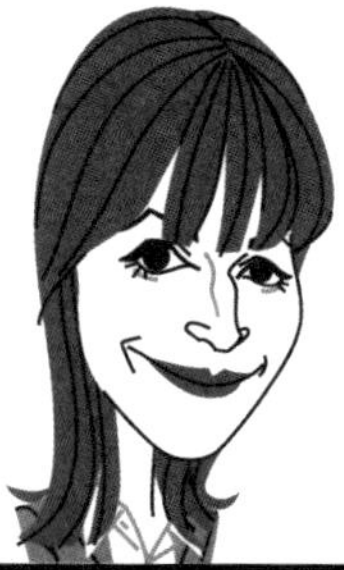

JESSICA WALSH

Jessica Walsh is a multidisciplinary designer working in New York City. Her work has won design awards from the Type Director's Club, Art Director's Club, SPD, Print, and Graphis. She has received various celebrated distinctions such as Computer Art's "Top Rising Star in Design," an Art Director's Club "Young Gun," and Print Magazine's "New Visual Artist".

POSTERS & PORTFOLIO

THE POSTERS

These posters will be exhibited at various locations in the United States and at our stores in the San Francisco Bay Area. They can be purchased directly through PUBLIC at publicbikes.com in both 40 x 60 inches and 20 x 30 inches sizes in both framed and unframed configurations. The website contains greater information about the designers and related PUBLIC WORKS products.

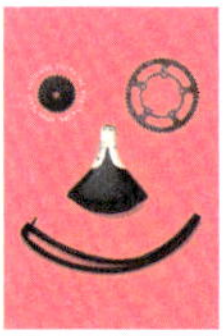

1

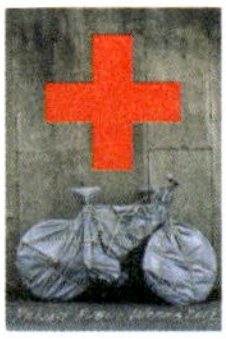

2

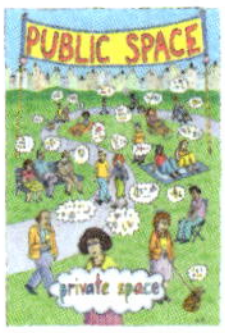

3

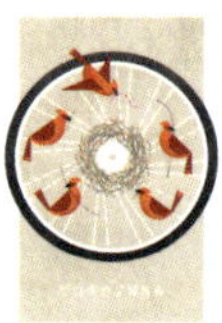

4

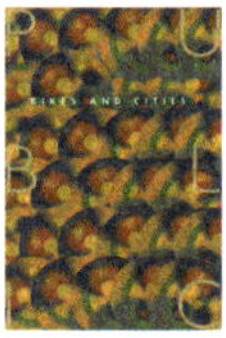

5

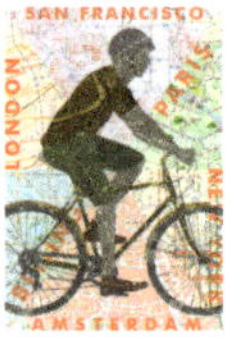

6

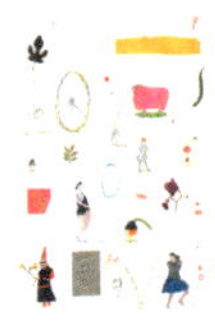

7

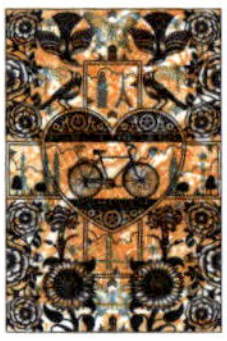

8

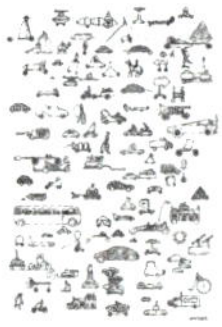

9

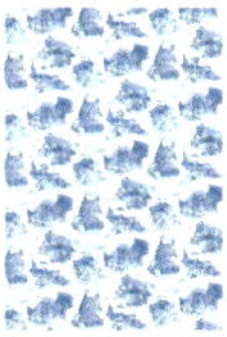

10

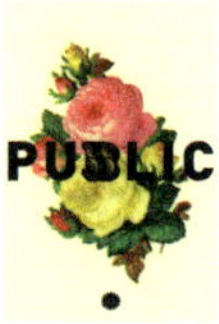

11

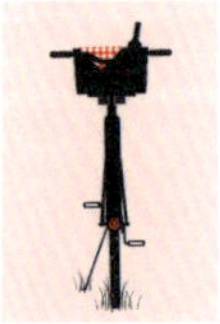

12

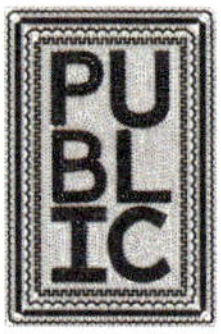

13

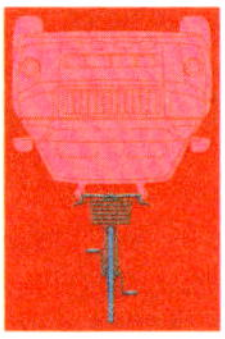

14

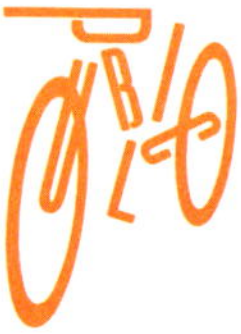

15

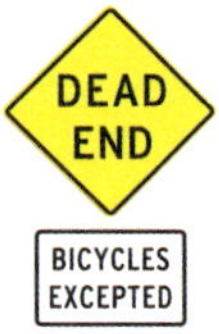

16

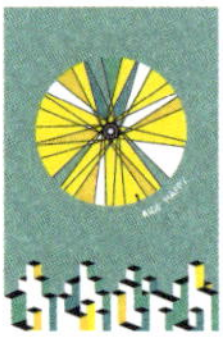

17

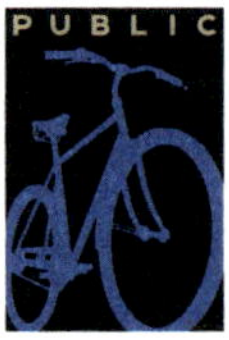

18

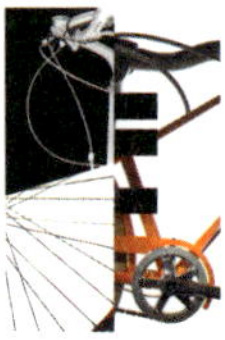

19

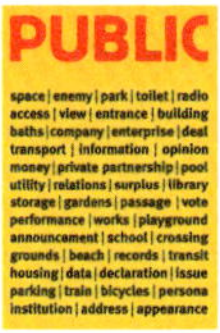

20

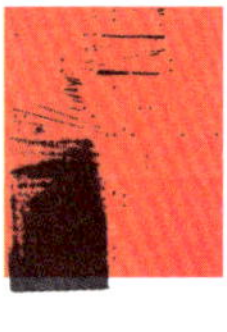

21

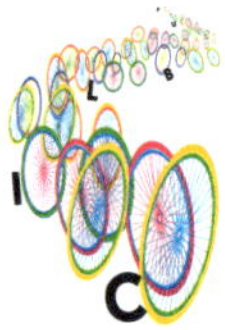

22

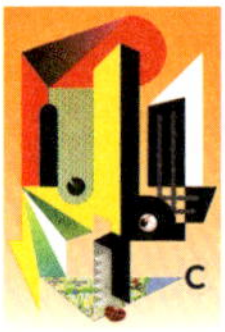

23

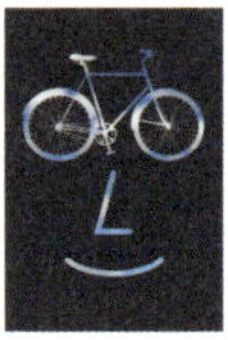

24

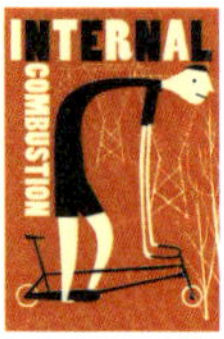

25

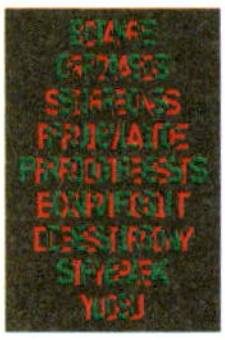

26

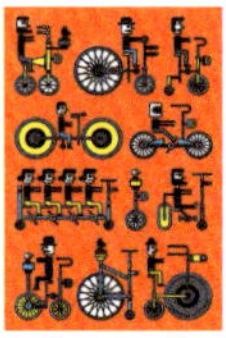

27

INDIVIDUAL POSTERS

20 x 30 inches (50.8x76.2 cm) $50.00 USD*

40 x 60 inches (101.6x152.4 cm) $350.00 USD*

Signed edition available on request

at design@publicbikes.com

*Note: Prices are subject to change.

THE PORTFOLIO COLLECTION

These twenty-seven 20 x 30 inch (50.8 x 76.2 cm) posters are available in a signed or an unsigned edition on archival paper in a special collectors portfolio. Special prices are available on request for schools and other institutions. For more information, please visit us at publicbikes.com or call 888-450-0123.

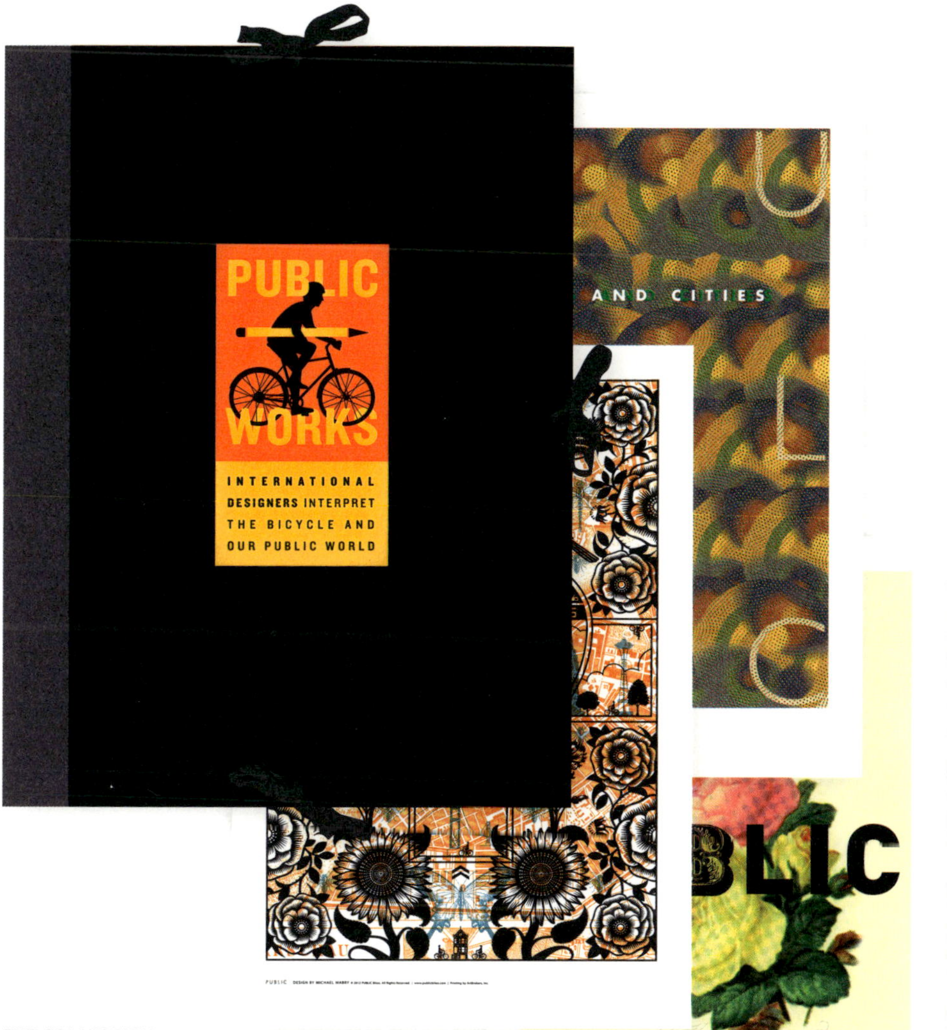

THE COLLECTION

Complete Signed Collection
in Portfolio $2,500
Complete Unsigned Collection
in Portfolio $1,500

*Note: Prices are subject to change.

INDEX